Presented to

_____

By

_____

On the Occasion of

_____

Date

_____

Lord, I Need Your Blessing

SEEKING, FINDING, AND APPRECIATING GOD'S GOODNESS

ANITA CORRINE DONIHUE

BARBOUR
PUBLISHING

Published by Barbour Publishing, Inc., P.O. Box 719, Uhrichsville, Ohio 44683, www.barbourbooks.com

Our mission is to publish and distribute inspirational products offering exceptional value and biblical encouragement to the masses.

 Member of the
Evangelical Christian
Publishers Association

Printed in the United States of America.
5 4 3 2 1

Dedicated with love to

my son Timothy.

Contents

INTRODUCTION

Lord, I need Your blessing. And I need it now!

How often have I longingly come to You in desperation and prayed to You this way? How often have I asked for Your blessings under *my* terms? In *my* timing?

Do You hear me when I'm perplexed and don't know which way to turn? What about the times I just can't get things right? Are You able to bless me when I'm sick? What if I were dying? Would You still help me then?

When temptations, frustrations, stress, and sorrows press in on me from every side, I can barely imagine Your blessings. Do You care about me during those times, Lord? How I long for Your comfort and friendship through hours of loneliness and grief. Are You able to fill those gaping chasms in times like these? Where are Your blessings when life seems unfair?

Wait a minute, Lord. Is this the way You really want me to bring my needs to You? If instead of my asking, almost demanding, that everything be done my way, would it be better for me to willingly bow at Your footstool with an open, pliable heart?

I read in Haggai how Joshua, the high priest of Judah, honored You and put You first in his life. Yes, Lord. This is what I want to do. I will live for You above all else. Then as I do so, let me place my needs in Your hands. Show me, I pray, how to balance my priorities that I may be a blessing to You.

When I experience Your kindness, remind me to thank You, Lord. Teach me to notice the everyday blessings, big and small. Can I even number them all? I'm beginning to realize counting my blessings is a process. A *God-filled process* with You in charge. After all, You know what's best for me even better than I.

As I come before You in prayer, I ask You to bless me with Your holy, guiding presence. Here, Lord, I recall Your promise in the Bible: "From this day I will bless you" (Haggai 2:19 NKJV).

GENUINE JOY

Joy, Deep Within

The line of customers stretched from the fast-food restaurant's front counter, past the door, and out onto the sidewalk. I barely had time to breathe, ringing up order after order, bagging, filling trays, smiling, and offering a "Have a great evening." This was only one of the many rushes I experienced in working my second job.

The line began to shorten. Near the end of the rush, I noticed a pleasant-looking gentleman waiting patiently. It was refreshing to see after serving so many hurried customers.

Soon the man arrived at the counter and gave me his order. Then he looked me in the eyes. "What makes you so happy? You must be tired and your feet probably hurt."

"I am, and they do. But I'm happy because I'm a Christian and I have a joy deep inside my heart."

The man nodded and gave a huge grin. "I knew it. I just knew it! I'm a Christian, too. I could feel the Spirit of the Lord about you as I watched you work. Keep on keeping on, dear sister!

That event pressed itself deep into my memory.

When troubles and discouragements crowd in, we can draw on an immeasurable, life-fulfilling joy God provides deep within our souls.

What sunshine is to flowers, smiles are to humanity.
These are but trifles, to be sure; but, scattered along life's
pathway, the good they do is inconceivable.
JOSEPH ADDISON, 1672–1719

Bask in the Son

We have a plant in our home that is a silent blessing to our family. It's called a "prayer plant." When I purchased it several years ago, it was in a small, four-inch pot. I placed it near a northeast window where it could bask in the early morning sun. I never gave it much care. I simply watered it when I remembered and occasionally added some plant food. When the little plant grew, I transferred it to a larger pot.

It eventually matured enough to produce small, starlike white blossoms. And it just kept growing. Our prayer plant could only be described as a "happy plant." Its broad leaves gave off a lustrous beauty. In the evening, the leaves began coupling and pointing upward—a reminder of hands giving praise to our Creator. At daybreak, they spread out flat—a reminder of palms outstretched, offering submission to God.

Again, I moved the plant to a larger pot. It grew to the point where we had trouble finding space for it in our home. I finally moved it to the living room coffee table. Before long its broad leaves drooped. Bob and I realized the plant wasn't getting the sunlight it needed.

Now we have our prayer plant on our dining room table, once more in a northeast window. It has grown to about one foot high and over two feet wide! When friends and company come by, God uses this plant to remind us of the love and joy He gives us.

O LORD of hosts,
Blessed is the man that trusteth in thee. . . .
I will bless the LORD at all times:
His praise shall continually be in my mouth.
My soul shall make her boast in the LORD:
The humble shall hear thereof, and be glad.
O magnify the LORD with me,
and let us exalt his name together. . . .
Every day will I bless thee;
and I will praise thy name for ever and ever.
PSALMS 84:12; 34:1–3; 145:2 KJV

Where Do We Find Joy?

Where do we find joy in this fast-paced world of stress, greed, and uncertainty? Must the darkness of sin and discouragement overshadow everything in our lives? Look to the Son—the Son of God. Bask in His presence as often or more than you enjoy a good meal or television program. Draw near to the Son of God, and experience the way He causes us to bloom into happy, healthy Christians. *He* is our light and life.

Invite Jesus, the Son of God, into your heart. Feed on the words in His Bible. Like the prayer plant, stretch out your hands and lift your heart to Him in praise and thanksgiving. Mentally place your concerns, your wants, your needs, and your goals into your palms, and relinquish each one to Him. Ask for His forgiveness. Bask in the love that comes from the Son—the Son of God. Don't just do this once. Do it again and again.

When you do, you take the first step toward experiencing a good measure of God's joy and blessings being poured into your lap—pressed down, shaken together, and running over.

Light tomorrow with today.
ELIZABETH BARRETT BROWNING, 1806–1861

Indescribable Joy

Father, in the past I've looked for joy in many different places. Each time I found it to be shallow, conditional, and temporary. Circumstances and people constantly disappointed me. Good times and material belongings didn't give me complete joy.

It was when I turned my heart over to You that I found real joy. You continually place it deep within my soul. This joy comes from Your presence and remains with me through the good and bad in life.

Thank You for Your love, Father, and for Your indescribable joy.

You will show me the path of life;
In Your presence is fullness of joy;
At Your right hand are pleasures forevermore.
PSALM 16:11 NKJV

The Half Has Never Been Told

I know I love Thee better, Lord,
Than any earthly joy.
For Thou hast given me the peace
Which nothing can destroy.

I know that Thou art nearer still
Than any earthly throng,
And sweeter is the thought of Thee
Than any lovely song.

The half has never yet been told,
Of love so full and free;
The half has never yet been told.
His blood—it cleanseth me.

FRANCES RIDLEY HAVERGAL, 1836–1879

Oh, what endless, infinite joy we find in the love of Jesus!
—It's a God-filled process!

FINDING FREEDOM

True Freedom

Many of us think freedom is being able to go, do, and say what we want. Others long for freedoms we take for granted. Throughout history, innumerable people have given everything for this cause.

But there's a different kind of freedom. It's a liberation from sin's oppression brought on by others or ourselves. This true freedom was purchased for each of us by Jesus, the Son of God. With a power beyond our imagination and comprehension, He took mankind's sins upon Himself and freed us from the bondage of Satan. When we accept Jesus, we find that freedom through Him is the key to life itself. This is when the blessings begin to flow!

Jesus said to them, "You are truly my disciples if you live as I tell you to, and you will know the truth, and the truth will set you free. . . . You are slaves of sin, every one of you. And slaves don't have rights, but the Son has every right there is! So if the Son sets you free, you will indeed be free."
JOHN 8:31–32, 34–36 TLB

Never Too Late

Leslie* grew up in a Christian family. She enjoyed an idyllic home life with her parents and grandparents setting fine Christian examples. When she was three days old, her family wrapped her snugly in a blanket and carted her off to church. There her family carried Leslie to the church altar where they prayed with their minister and dedicated her to the Lord. What could be better? She learned all the usual Bible verses, walked the Christian walk, and talked the Christian talk. She was "all right" with God. Surely He would keep blessing her. After all, she was a Christian because of her family heritage. Or was she?

At age nineteen, Leslie discovered a freedom she had never experienced before—the freedom of doing what she wanted as an adult. The catch was, she also had to make important decisions. She often felt an incredible tug-of-war going on over what was right and wrong. She experienced tremendous pressure from coworkers at her part-time job and from some new friends at college. Did she have the strength to live the way her parents had always taught her?

Leslie began running with the wrong crowd. Soon, she was drinking heavily and experimenting with drugs. She found herself staying out later and later, and she began having trouble at school and work. One night after a party, the police pulled Leslie over and arrested her for drunk driving. She realized she'd made a mess of everything. Where was the happiness she'd once experienced?

She knew if she didn't catch up with her studies, she would be kicked out of college. Her family's disappointment in her was beyond words. Leslie wanted God to bless her work, her goals, and her dreams for the future. Where was God now when she needed Him the most?

Some of her fellow college students kept asking her to party. But Mark was different. She often sat near him in her Creative Writing class. Since Leslie needed help with her work, she joined Mark and a couple of other students in a study group. During their study times, Leslie discovered Mark was a Christian. Surprisingly, so were the other two students in the group. After poring over their books, the conversation sometimes drifted toward how each one felt about God.

"Well, um, sure, I'm a Christian." Leslie faltered. "I've grown up in a Christian home."

Mark rolled his eyes and sighed. "Leslie, living in

a Christian home doesn't make you a Christian any more than going to pro basketball games makes you a professional ballplayer! You have to decide for yourself. No wonder you're having so much trouble in your life. God can only bless you if you ask Jesus personally to become your Savior."

Leslie slumped in her chair. "But I've blown it. God doesn't want now, after the way I've messed up."

Mark took her hand. "It's never too late to ask Him into your life, Leslie."

Leslie's three new friends prayed with her as she asked Jesus to become Lord of her life. She hadn't become a Christian because she was raised that way, but because she made a personal choice to follow Him.

Life was different from then on. Leslie discovered a joy and relationship in the Lord she had never experienced before. Temptations were much easier to overcome with God helping her. Her grades improved.

Her relationship with her family was restored. God blessed her with a successful career. And Mark? God blessed Leslie beyond her dreams. She and Mark became more than friends. They became husband and wife. Now Mark and Leslie are also raising their children to love and serve God.

Leslie is telling everyone who will listen how he or she can find a new kind of freedom and be wonderfully blessed by God, and that it's never too late to start.

*Name changed.

A moment's insight is sometimes worth a life's experience.
OLIVER WENDELL HOLMES, 1809–1894

The Freedom of Forgiveness

Thirty-year-old Jerry loved his grandfather, Harold, more than he could express. Since Jerry's grandmother had died several years earlier, Jerry knew how much his grandfather needed his love and friendship. Harold was young for his age, possessing an enthusiasm for life not often seen in an elderly man. Because of this, Jerry and Harold enjoyed traveling, fishing, and sometimes just watching television together. They had much in common and became very good friends, in addition to enjoying their roles as grandfather and grandson.

Jerry's grandfather became involved with a woman in her late twenties. The woman convinced Harold she loved him. Before long, the older man was hopelessly smitten. No amount of reasoning on Jerry's part helped change his grandfather's mind. The relationship between grandson and grandfather grew terribly strained, especially after Harold married the woman.

It turned out she and her family were part of a huge sweetheart-scam organization. Harold lost his home and all of his savings. Jerry could do nothing to stop this horrible process. Unfortunately, the unscrupulous woman and her cohorts managed to escape any consequences of the law. In spite of everything, Jerry remained close to his grandfather and helped him in every way possible. He knew it was the right thing to do.

Jerry prayed fervently that his grandfather would be released from the conniving family. But they stuck to Harold like leeches. After a time, Jerry's grandfather couldn't take the emotional pressure of the family's constant badgering. Brokenhearted, he passed away.

The woman and her family left the area and were not to be found. They had taken all they could from Harold. Now they would move on to other unsuspecting older people.

Jerry experienced feelings of rage. He thought about ways he could get even. Yet he knew this wasn't the way God wanted him to feel. He recognized that unless he left the whole thing to the Lord, he would become a prisoner of his own anger and bitterness. What had been done would never be right. But he knew he must forgive those who wronged his grandfather as Jesus had forgiven him.

With the Lord's help and the help of good Christian friends, Jerry found a tool that set him free from his bondage: He learned to pray for the salvation of those who had wronged his grandfather. No matter where they went or what they did, his prayers would follow. He asked the Holy Spirit to constantly keep after them for the rest of their lives, so they would turn their hearts over to Christ.

Jerry changed his fury to forgiveness by leaving everything in God's hands. He eventually found peace and victory. Jerry may never know the good that God will accomplish through his Christian example. It doesn't matter. God knows. And He has a way of working all circumstances together for good when we trust and obey Him.

I bless the holy name of God with all my heart. Yes,
I will bless the Lord and not forget the glorious things
he does for me. He forgives all my sins. He heals me.
He ransoms me from [a life of destruction]. He surrounds
me with lovingkindness and tender mercies.
He fills my life with good things!
My youth is renewed like the eagle's!
PSALM 103:1–5 TLB

I do not consider myself yet to have taken hold of it.
But one thing I do: Forgetting what is behind and
straining toward what is ahead, I press on toward the
goal to win the prize for which God has called me
heavenward in Christ Jesus.
PHILIPPIANS 3:13–14 NIV

Freedom through You

Father, I always thought You would bless me because You are God. It made sense to me. After all, You are all-loving and can do anything to fix things. This is how I felt until a friend showed me in Your Bible that every one of us has sinned and has fallen short of Your glory and blessings. I began to realize I couldn't have it both ways. To You, being a good person wasn't enough. I would either serve the devil or the Lord.

Before I gave You everything, I felt a bondage in my life. Even though I tried to do the right things, I couldn't understand what it meant to be unshackled from the awful burdens sin causes. I had no idea what it was like to experience Your marvelous presence and help. I finally learned what this freedom so many Christians referred to was all about and how I could have it in my life.

I asked You to come into my heart, to forgive my sins, and become my Lord and Savior. And You did. When I gave You my life, my all, I felt such a sweet relief. Amazingly, You didn't stop there. You went on to show me how to forgive others like You forgave me. The burdens of sin, bitterness, and anger rolled away.

How excited I am about giving my heart to You. Everywhere I go, I feel compelled to tell people about my decision to love and serve You. There's a wonderful peace and contentment deep inside me that I had never felt before. There's a freedom that has replaced the bondage I once experienced. You are the Way, the Truth, and the Life, Lord. Now that I know Your truth, I am set free from the burden of sin; and each day is full of wonderful adventures with You as my Savior and Guide.

You are all sons [and daughters] of God through faith in Christ Jesus.
GALATIANS 3:26 NIV

All in Jesus

There is peace and joy in the Lord today,
More than all in this world of sin;
There's a happy life in the holy way,
Praise the Lord, I have entered in!

I am blest today, I am free indeed,
What a pleasure to serve the Lord!
How it fills my soul with delight to read
In His sacred and holy Word!

Praise the Lord, I am free in His love and grace!
Oh, His blood reaches me!
I abide 'neath His smiling face.

BARNEY ELLIOTT WARREN, 1867–1951

God's liberating power breaks our
fetters and allows us to soar.
—It's a God-filled process!

MENTAL MOTIVATION

A New Mind-Set

One of the most exciting experiences in my life was when I totally dedicated my life to the Lord at the age of eighteen. I had accepted Jesus as my Savior when I was seven years old, while attending an after-school Child Evangelism group. I now realize that was only my first step.

As I reached adulthood, God revealed to me that He had much more to offer. Before then, He wasn't the first and foremost person in my life. Although I had become a Christian, I wanted to do things my own way, in my timing. Through the influence of our church's youth pastor, God showed me a better way to *really* live. God taught me how to walk and talk with Him day by day. I quickly learned He required something from me far more important than talent. He wanted my unconditional obedience. I soon began to experience His presence all the time, everywhere I went. His Spirit spoke to my spirit. His love intertwined throughout my life. One step at a time, God gave me a new mind-set regarding my goals and dreams. He gave me a different purpose for the future—one centered in His will.

A brand-new adventure began—an adventure that will never end. I enrolled in college. I began to seriously study the scriptures. New dreams, goals, and discoveries opened before me like a holy carpet rolled out by God. As I now walk along His carpeted path, I discover the things He has planned for me far exceed my wildest dreams.

Sometimes, I allow negative circumstances to bog me down. I begin to develop an attitude of discouragement and oppression. Whenever this happens, however, God stops me at a checkpoint along His pathway and draws me back to His optimistic, constructive mindset. He does this through the influence of my faithful Christian friends, my husband, my reading of the Bible, and His Holy Spirit ministering to my soul.

I'm thankful God constantly reminds me that life is worth living. I want to grow and learn more every day. Today is a new day. Today, I look forward as He renews my mind-set and takes me on another adventure with Him.

Our goals are our possibilities.
ROBERT BROWNING, 1812–1889

A Vision Passed On

Young Charles Booth was filled to the brim with enthusiasm and ambition. His Christian parents passed down values to their son to work hard and learn as much as possible. Charles's mother passed away when he was a child. His father suffered many years from poor health. Charles worked on farms and in warehouses to earn money. Little did he know his experiences would help map his future.

In college, Charles soon found a passion to teach and counsel students. One instructor, Mary Simpson, helped set a platform for his future teaching method: to show genuine concern for young people and motivate them to do their best. She often stated, "The most important element in the classroom is the student."

During summers, Charles worked construction jobs in Alaska to pay for the education he loved. In a few years, he earned his bachelor's and master's degrees in education, majoring in psychology and counseling.

After college, he married his sweetheart, Leila; and the couple launched their teaching careers, guiding students from all walks of life. Charles immediately applied the valued lessons from Mary Simpson to the classroom.

To stimulate his students' desire to learn, he provided an advanced class in literature. He also loved teaching students who experienced difficulty in achieving. He became a high school counselor.

Charles later accepted a position as director of pupil services for the school district, where he then reorganized the functions of the special education department and helped implement alternative educational and curriculum developments. Before long, Charles became the district's assistant superintendent, then deputy superintendent.

Charles's life then took a surprising turn. People encouraged him to run for office. As mayor, Charles supported the building of a mall and helped refine the rail transit system. He organized the start of alternative high schools, reentry programs for at-risk students and those with special needs, and many other training centers.

He served on the boards and committees of numerous civic organizations that supported and focused on educational and mental health needs of the community's youth, including drug education and mental retardation. He also served with the state's oldest child welfare organization.

Charles has received awards for his outstanding community service and leadership, as well as the Distinguished Alumni Award from Central Washington

University Alumni Association. He and Leila have received citizenship and "everyday hero" awards.

Charles still loves to hear from his former students. Many live productive lives. Some are teachers. Others have doctorate degrees. A few serve in politics.

During his "retirement," Charles is rereading the early Greek and Roman literature and the classics he taught to eager students years ago. He still serves on many city and county boards and committees, and he continues to motivate young people.

Charles's and Leila's service to their church has always been unique. For ten years he enjoyed doing the church's landscaping and gardening. While he was mayor, Charles and Leila enjoyed their summers visiting every church in the community. They are still involved in their local church and sing in the choir.

Charles believes it's important to care about how people feel. He says, "Life is too short to cause grief. Listening is one of the best steps toward getting things accomplished. It's important to honor each person as a valuable individual and maintain his or her dignity. It helps the battles of the will to dissolve and makes a way for people to work together."

At times we wonder why life takes different turns. Charles and Leila Booth are living proof that God can use life experiences to pass on a vision to those who follow—a vision to help make this world a better place in which to live.

Work hard so God can say to you, "Well done." Be a good workman, one who does not need to be ashamed when God examines your work. Know what his Word says and means. . . .

Don't be conceited, sure of your own wisdom. Instead, trust and reverence the Lord, and turn your back on evil; when you do that, then you will be given renewed health and vitality. . . .

For wisdom and truth will enter the very center of your being, filling your life with joy.

2 TIMOTHY 2:15; PROVERBS 3:7–8; 2:10 TLB

The Child of Knowledge

Wise men ever know their own ignorance and are ready to learn. Humility is the child of knowledge. Michaelangelo was found by the Cardinal Farnese walking in solitude amid the ruins of the Coliseum. When the Cardinal expressed his surprise, the great artist answered, "I go yet to school that I may continue to learn."

CHARLES H. SPURGEON, 1834–1892

The Bridge-Builder

An old man, going a lone highway
Came at the evening, cold and gray.
To a chasm vast and wide and steep,
With waters rolling cold and deep.
The old man crossed in the twilight dim;
The sullen stream had no fears for him.
But he turned when safe on the other side,
And built a bridge to span the tide.

"Old man," said a fellow pilgrim near,
"You are wasting your strength with building here.
Your journey will end with the ending day,
You never again will pass this way.
You've crossed the chasm, deep and wide,
Why build you this bridge at eventide?"
The builder lifted his old gray head.
"Good friend, in the path I have come," he said,

"There followed after me today
A youth whose feet must pass this way.
The chasm that was as naught to me
To that fair-haired youth may a pitfall be;
He, too, must cross in the twilight dim—
Good friend, I am building this bridge for him."

WILL ALLEN DROMGOOLE, 1860–1934

Renew My Mind-Set, Lord

Renew my mind-set, Lord, so it will be in compliance with Your will. Remind me to heed Your instruction that motivates my mind and makes life worth living. Help me to be open-minded to what You are teaching me through Your scriptures.

Bless me as I seek wise counsel in making decisions. May I be flexible when I'm being shown how to correct my errors. I want to present myself a living offering to You, O Lord, putting You first in my life.

When I'm tempted to compromise my standards and conform to the things of this world rather than Your will, renew my mind, I pray. In so doing, may I be living proof of what is good and acceptable in accordance with Your perfect will. You haven't given me a spirit of uncertainty and fear. You have given me a spirit of power and love and a sound mind.

Let it be so, Lord. My mind-set is in You! Amen.

I beseech you therefore, brethren, by the mercies of God, that you present your bodies a living sacrifice, holy, acceptable to God, which is your reasonable service. And do not be conformed to this world, but be transformed by the renewing of your mind, that you may prove what is that good and acceptable and perfect will of God. . . .

For God has not given us a spirit of fear, but of power and of love and of a sound mind.

ROMANS 12:1–2; 2 TIMOTHY 1:7 NKJV

My Song Shall Be of Jesus

My song shall be of Jesus, when sitting at His feet,
I call to mind His goodness, in meditation sweet;
My song shall be of Jesus, whatever ill betide;
I'll sing the grace that saves me, and keeps me at His side.

FANNY CROSBY, 1820–1915

A positive mind-set comes when we allow
God to subtract despair and add hope.
—It's a God-filled process!

DAILY DECISIONS

Blessed Release

Do you love God but struggle with trusting Him for guidance regarding daily decisions? When you take things into your own hands, do you find yourself running in circles? Do things become more tangled than ever? Although you feel you have forgiven others and yourself, do hurts, distress, bitterness, and anger eat away at you like a deadly cancer? Here is a family who felt this way.

Donna* and her husband, Ben, interlocked arms and shuffled across the sand toward the ocean waves. They had awakened early after a restless night's sleep at a nearby hotel. A walk on the beach would calm their emotions. When they reached the water's edge, chilly, salt-laced air filled their nostrils. Without speaking, they watched tiny diamondlike stars fade into the slate gray sky. Donna offered a silent prayer of thanks for their much-needed retreat.

Ben gave Donna's hand a gentle squeeze. "I'm going for a run."

Donna nodded and watched him jog away. Recent stress brought on by their twenty-year-old son Guy had taken its toll on their marriage. Donna thought about the heartbreaking event from the night before and shuddered. Guy's angry, accusing words spewed at her over the phone. How many times had he talked this way?

Whenever they rescued Guy from self-caused predicaments, he took their help and disappeared. If they refused, he made them feel guilty.

They could see good things in their son. But he had recently chosen the wrong friends. Instead of being the leader, Guy was following a road to disaster. Donna recalled past times when Guy talked about his love for the Lord. In spite of everything, she could still see glimmers of hope for him.

But how could she and Ben break through the barriers? Stinging tears welled in Donna's eyes. At least she could pray. She remembered a different phone conversation she'd had with her dad.

"Give it to God," her father had gently advised. She pondered his words and looked out to where the waves met the western sky. Then she gritted her teeth and shouted a prayer: "What will become of our family, Lord? Why is this happening? Do You hear my prayer above the waves?" She dropped to her knees on the sand. Her neck felt stiff. Her joints ached from lack of sleep. She had tried everything. Now she had no other choice but to listen to her Lord.

Soon God began ministering to her open heart.

Give Me your past.

Agony swept through her at the thought of Guy's rebellious years. She hung her head in shame, recalling mistakes she and Ben had made. She watched the tide recede. Each wave carried away debris, leaving smooth, clean sand. Bible verses came to mind: *"Once again you will have compassion on us. You will tread our sins beneath your feet; you will throw them into the depths of the ocean! You will bless us as you promised Jacob long ago"* (Micah 7:19–20 TLB).

Donna stood and began walking. Before long, she felt something irritating her toes. She limped toward a log and removed her sandals. Tiny grains of sand had lodged between her toes. Sandals in hand, she stepped into a puddle and rinsed her feet in the cold, invigorating salt water. Discomfort left. A chill zipped through her.

Give Me your pain and anger.

"Lord, I've already forgiven Guy." Her voice cracked with emotion. "But the hurt won't go away." She broke into uncontrollable sobs. As long as she harbored hurts, she wasn't truly forgiving Guy or herself. Instead of feeling better, her heartaches only worsened. "Lord, take *Your* cleansing water and rinse away my resentment. Bury it in Your deepest sea."

Be still, and know that I am God, she felt Him whisper.

She shuffled to dry sand and sat down. As each sorrow came to mind, Donna reached for a handful of sand. She extended her arm, opened her palm, and let the wind carry the sand away. Bitterness peeled from her heart like foul-smelling layers of onion. Relief and freedom swept over her in a way she hadn't experienced in years. "Thank You, Lord," she whispered.

Give Me your present.

Donna cringed. "No matter how much I try, everything results in disaster." She knew she must trust God to deal with her son through His own methods and timing. The Lord was always able to speak to Guy's heart. By trying to fix things, she may well have gotten in the way of God's working directly with her son. Nothing was too hard for Him! He was her advocate and could solve any problems.

Donna drew herself to her full height and boldly shouted His promise in 1 John 4:4: "Greater is He who is in you than he who is in the world!" (NASB).

Seagulls skillfully glided on the wind. With precise movements, they dove for fish. Had they learned from trial and error? She recalled how eagles taught their young to fly by taking them up on powerful wings and letting them go. The eaglets frantically flapped their wings and flew a short distance. Then, like Guy, some started to fall. But at that moment, the adult eagles swooped under the babies and caught them on their wings. The mighty birds repeated the exercise until the eaglets were strong enough to fly on their own.

Donna's voice lowered to a whisper. "Lord, Guy is like a little bird being pushed from the nest." Even so, she would not doubt God. She could be there for Guy and *care*, but not *do*. "When he falls, Lord, I trust You to catch him and teach him to grow stronger."

She smiled as she pondered another one of God's promises: *"But they that wait upon the LORD shall renew their strength; they shall mount up with wings as eagles; they shall run, and not be weary; and they shall walk, and not faint"* (Isaiah 40:31 KJV).

"What about the financial disaster we're facing, Lord? We have paid out so much in trying to help our son. Now we have nothing left except bills. What shall we do?"

Give Me your belongings.

Another verse from His Word floated across her mind: *"Seek first his kingdom and his righteousness, and all these things will be given to you as well"* (Matthew 6:33 NIV).

She studied the gnarled trees and weather-beaten wildflowers, surrounded by dry, amber beach grass in the dunes. How many storms had they survived? Since the Lord provided for His handiwork, surely He would help her family.

"Grant us strength, Lord, to put You before our belongings and finances. Help us to recover from this terrible ordeal. Help us to not be enablers. Teach us instead to trust in You."

Give Me your future.

Peace filled Donna as she began to visualize a light at the end of the tunnel. She knew that Christ, the solid Rock, would help her and Ben build their future on His sure foundation. She pondered at how her feet had clumsily sunk in the sand when she and Ben first walked the beach. Again she called out to God, "You are my Rock and my strength, Lord! I trust You to go before and behind me. In You I believe!"

As she looked down the beach, Donna could see Ben running toward her. He greeted her with a broad smile. "Donna," he blurted, "I just gave all of our problems to God." He took a deep breath and continued. "The Lord has control. He'll help us through."

The couple united in prayer for their son, their needs, and dreams for their future.

Guy soon noticed the change in his parents. Healing and forgiveness replaced the tug-of-war between parents and son. Guy recommitted his life to the Lord. Because Ben and Donna had released everything to God, He was able to bless their family more than they ever dreamed.

*Names changed.

For the LORD loves the just
and will not forsake his faithful ones. . . .
"So do not fear,
for I am with you;
do not be dismayed,
for I am your God.
I will strengthen you and help you;
I will uphold you with my righteous right hand."
. . . God has said,
"Never will I leave you;
never will I forsake you."

PSALM 37:28; ISAIAH 41:10; HEBREWS 13:5 NIV

The Nudge

People in the small town were going about their business as usual—waving to friends and taking turns at the four-way-stop intersection. Then, without warning, traffic halted in all directions.

A little lady in her eighties, walking in the middle of the street, caused heads to turn and mouths to gape. She wore a floppy garden hat and a large apron that wrapped around her simple housedress. In one hand, she carried a broom. In the other, she firmly gripped the handle of a large galvanized garbage can lid and held it like a shield. She carefully kept both items between her and a slow-moving possum.

Step by step, she nudged the critter with the broom. Once in a while it stopped, glanced back, and gave her a dirty look. This never deterred the woman. She gently but firmly kept pushing the possum forward.

She acted like she had dealt with this animal or others like it before. Folks began carefully driving around her, not sure if they wanted to become involved. No one got out and offered his or her help. A police officer slammed on his brakes in total surprise. After assessing the situation, he, too, drove on.

Finally, after a three-block trek, the lady managed to guide the possum into a nearby grove of bushes and trees. Then she turned abruptly and walked back the way she had come.

Most people don't want to bother with such a homely, offensive little creature as a possum. But this lady had enough compassion to do so. In the same way, there are times when we find people straying from the path God wants them to walk. Some folks don't look so great. Others might even be offensive. But God still loves them. He may ask us to take our time to care about them. Although it often requires determination and patience on our part, He'll show us how to gently and firmly nudge them closer to Him. As we allow Him to interrupt our daily routines and push us out of our comfort zones, God often provides us with surprising blessings.

Your ears will hear a word behind you, "This is the
way, walk in it," whenever you turn to the right
*   or to the left. . . .*
I will instruct you and teach you in the way which
*   you should go;*
I will counsel you with My eye upon you. . . .
For such is God,
Our God forever and ever;
He will guide us until death.
ISAIAH 30:21; PSALMS 32:8; 48:14 NASB

God loves us. He never gives up on us.
        —It's a God-filled process!

Decision's Process

Father, I have wrestled for days with this decision I'm forced to deal with. No matter which way I turn, I'm unable to come up with an answer. I've tried seeking counsel from people I respect. Unfortunately, I receive all kinds of answers. I realize I need godly wisdom that can only come from You. Please show me the right way to go.

As I seek Your will, I'm learning there's a process in making wise choices. Thank You for guiding me with timeless answers in Your Word. Somehow, You manage to help me step back, take a deep breath, and with an open mind learn everything I can involving this situation.

I place my faith in You that everything will work out according to Your will. All I need to do is follow Your lead, one step, one day at a time. Thank You now for placing an adviser in my path who is informed, wise, and, most of all, an honest, dedicated Christian.

As I go through this decision-making process, I'm learning that I'm not the ultimate answer to the problem. I'm limited in what I can do. But You, Lord, are all-knowing. Your abilities to provide a solution are unlimited!

Now, I come to You, asking for help and guidance. In You, I put my total trust. I will not allow a shadow of doubt to hinder what You are about to accomplish. You have shown me that doubts are like a wave in the ocean, driven and tossed recklessly in the wind.

I praise You for direction and for granting me peace of heart and mind. In all circumstances, I trust and obey You, Lord. I can already see how You are blessing and working things out in the way You know is best.

How blessed is the man who finds wisdom
And the man who gains understanding.
For her profit is better than the profit of silver
And her gain better than fine gold. . . .
Trust in the LORD with all your heart
And do not lean on your own understanding.
In all your ways acknowledge Him,
And He will make your paths straight.

PROVERBS 3:13–14, 5–6 NASB

Our Father in Heaven, Creator of All

Our Father in heaven, Creator of all,
O Source of all wisdom, on Thee would we call;
Thou only canst teach us, and show us our need,
And give to Thy children true knowledge indeed,
And give to Thy children true knowledge indeed.

But vain our instruction and blind must we be,
Unless with our learning be knowledge of Thee;
Then pour forth Thy Spirit, and open our eyes,
And fill with the knowledge that only makes wise,
And fill with the knowledge that only makes wise.
Amen.

THOMAS WISTAR, 1764–1851

Honey from the honeycomb is sweet to
your lips and gives nourishment.
Wisdom from God is sweet to your
soul and gives discernment.
—It's a God-filled process!

BLESSINGS FROM
BLUNDERS

Trust—No Matter What!

When Linda stepped into her backyard, it was a normal, slightly overcast Seattle spring day. The air smelled fresh from an early rain and was full of the fragrance of flowers. Mother and father birds chirped energetically in the distance. One of their offspring quietly peeped for its food from the confines of a nearby birdhouse. Linda slipped on her gardening gloves. She glanced down at her cat, Tinker, and gently stroked her head. Tinker emitted an affectionate *meow* and rubbed against Linda's leg. Across the yard, a baby bird clumsily fluttered from the birdhouse to a fence.

Linda had barely begun her gardening when a streak of fur shot past her toward the fence. It was Tinker. The cat grabbed the tiny bird with her teeth.

Linda lunged at the cat. "Oh, no, you don't!" she shouted firmly. In one swift move, she grabbed the cat and loosened her jaws. The fledgling slipped from Linda's garden gloves, fell to the ground, and frantically hopped through a hole in the neighbor's fence. Tinker's dejected look and laid-back ears made it clear how she felt about the whole thing.

Before Linda could take a breath, the neighbor's cat darted back through the hole in the fence, bird in mouth. Linda lunged again.

"Aha," she muttered. "Gotcha!" She managed to again retrieve the little bird and hold on to it. The neighbor's cat slinked back to his home. Linda gently lifted the bird to its house and slipped it inside. "Now stay there," she urged.

Would the parents accept the bird that was now covered with smells of cat hair and garden gloves? Linda wondered and waited. The parents returned with food for their young one. They flew around the birdhouse. After what seemed like forever, they slipped inside and gave their baby its much-needed food and comfort. Linda sighed with relief. Tinker looked at her quizzically, possibly wondering what she had done wrong.

How had Linda managed to perform such a rescue? She shook her head in surprise. What an amazing thing, the way that baby bird allowed her to handle it. What an amazing thing, the way the mother and father bird had enough trust in spite of strange odors from Linda's gloves to reunite with their baby. God really had been watching over that little bird.

*Written with permission from Linda Green.

His Hands

We often go through the mundane steps of our days at home, work, or school. We make what appear to us to be the wisest choices, hoping we are right. We marvel over near misses on the highways. We struggle with problems we can't solve. Some circumstances we face are beyond our control. Others may be frightening and heartbreaking. The world is too complex for us to figure out. But God is well aware of the entire picture. No matter what, He always knows what to do on our behalf.

Perhaps the birds in Linda's backyard knew her better than she realized and felt comfortable with her around. We have the privilege of being comfortable and secure in the presence of God. When we are so, we are able to completely put our trust in Him and place ourselves in His capable hands.

Pick Up My Puzzle Pieces

Lord, I feel everything I'm in involved in right now is like a jumble of puzzle pieces. This is definitely a bungled day! I am so perplexed. I don't understand what I've been doing to make things such a mess. What I want to do, I'm unable to do right. Out of frustration, I'm finding myself responding in a negative way. All that I'm trying to accomplish is turning into shambles.

My heart is right, Lord. I'm trying to center my perspective completely on You. But like an obsessed puzzle-solver, I want to jump into my situations—which are giant-sized messes, pieces strewn everywhere—and fit the parts together without looking at the big picture. When I'm tired or frustrated, my attempts to sort situations out in the right manner fail miserably. Here, in the middle of chaos, I should have the sense to step back and take a good look.

Lord, I'm calling on You for help. I realize I'm not seeing the complete picture You are trying to show me. Is it too late for You to undo the mess I've made? Go behind me, I pray. Help me set right any problems I have caused. Ease the tension. Mend hurt feelings. Please pick up the confusing puzzle pieces and fit them together for good, in accordance with Your will.

Now I'm taking a deep breath and relaxing, so You can direct me. Thank You for meeting my needs.

And, Lord, the next time I have a bungled day, I'll try to remember to step back a little sooner and allow You to show me how to arrange the pieces into a beautiful picture, honoring You.

In spite of my bungles, thank You for blessing me with Your patience and love.

Blessed are all those who put their trust in Him. . . .
He who heeds the word wisely will find good,
And whoever trusts in the LORD, happy is he. . . .
You will keep him in perfect peace,
Whose mind is stayed on You,
Because he trusts in You.
PSALM 2:12; PROVERBS 16:20; ISAIAH 26:3 NKJV

Trusting Jesus

Simply trusting every day,
Trusting through a stormy way;
Even when my faith is small,
Trusting Jesus, that is all.

Singing if my way is clear;
Praying if the path be drear;
If in danger, for Him call;
Trusting Jesus, that is all.

EDGAR PAGE STITES, 1836–1921

Countless blessings spring forth when the
hand of trust clasps the hand of God.
—It's a God-filled process!

GROWING THROUGH GRIEF

Why, Lord?

Suzanne and Travis trembled on unsteady feet at their son's burial site. Suzanne's thoughts spun. *No parent should outlive their child!* James was only forty-three years old—too young to die. But he suffered from Down syndrome and congenital heart problems. Suzanne and Travis held each other close and prayed, then stumbled toward their car. Suzanne looked back as they drove away. She felt as if she were abandoning her son. She shuddered and reminded herself that he was no longer in his fragile earthly body. Now he was with the Lord.

The couple marveled at how many lives their son had touched in such a positive way. How blessed they now felt to have the love and support of their family and friends during their time of sorrow. Flowers, kind letters, cards, and phone calls meant a lot to them. But nothing could take away the ache in their hearts.

Weeks passed. Suzanne felt terribly alone in her grief. She relived happy memories of James, especially the last time they were together. Her husband tried to comfort her, with little success. Suzanne managed to get through her days at work. Nights, however, became a time of dread. The numbness she felt gave way to relentless emotional and physical pain. Her chest hurt. Her heart pounded wildly. She often bolted up in bed from nightmares that she was dying. The doctor assured Suzanne her heart was all right. Her pain came from mourning the loss of one to whom she had given life.

One night, when Travis was away on a business trip, she awakened with a start. Her heart was hammering. Pain squeezed her chest as if chains were binding her. Suzanne gasped for breath. She felt like her life was being sucked away. She staggered to the living room and turned on a light. She had suffered like this before, but this was the worst.

"Breathe deeply," she whispered. "Jesus, help me. Please!"

In and out. In and out. Her breathing steadied. Her heartbeat returned to normal. The pain gradually lessened.

Suzanne glanced at the clenched fists in her lap. She forced her hands open and looked at her palms in horror. Her fingernails had caused her hands to bleed. Although grief counseling was helping her, she realized she had to take her sorrow to God and allow Him to comfort and heal her.

She choked back deep sobs. "Why, Lord? Why did James have to die instead of me? Children should always live longer than their parents. I miss him so.

Please help me through this."

God honored Suzanne's cry for help. He began walking her through her grief, one step at a time. He kept reminding her that although she and Travis were hurting, James was with Him. No longer did her son have to struggle. No more sickness or pain. Although she began feeling better physically, Suzanne still couldn't get past her grief. One morning during a quiet time with the Lord, she asked God once more to bring her through her sorrow. She opened her Bible to the story of Jesus praying in the Garden of Gethsemane. He, too, had grieved for others and Himself. Suzanne read:

And He was withdrawn from them about a stone's throw, and He knelt down and prayed, saying, "Father, if it is Your will, take this cup away from Me; nevertheless not My will, but Yours, be done." Then an angel appeared to Him from heaven, strengthening Him. And being in agony, He prayed more earnestly. Then His sweat became like great drops of blood falling down to the ground.

LUKE 22:41–44 NKJV

Again, a second time, He went away and prayed, saying, "O My Father, if this cup cannot pass away from Me unless I drink it, Your will be done."

MATTHEW 26:42 NKJV

"I have manifested Your name to the men whom You have given Me out of the world. They were Yours, You gave them to Me, and they have kept Your word. . . .

"I pray for them. . . . I do not pray that You should take them out of the world, but that You should keep them from the evil one."

JOHN 17:6, 9, 15 NKJV

Suzanne bowed her head. "Lord, I realize You used James's life to bless others in spite of his illness. Although I'm thankful he's in heaven with You, I haven't been willing to let him go. I submit to Your will and purpose in this. Even though I long for the sorrow to be removed from me, I relinquish to You my past, my future, my all."

A peace she hadn't experienced in a long time swept over Suzanne. She thought of how Jesus prayed in the Garden of Gethsemane for everyone who loved Him, including her. She felt God's comforting yet powerful Holy Spirit fill and surround her. She realized the same power that raised Jesus from the dead had set Christians free from sin and given them a wonderful eternal life with Him!

Suzanne opened her Bible to another promise: "But He was wounded for our transgressions, He was bruised for our iniquities; the chastisement for our peace was upon Him, and by His stripes we are healed" (Isaiah 53:5 NKJV).

"Thank You for taking care of my son, Lord. Thank You for the way You are healing me. I'm willing to give my sorrow to You and allow You to show me my purpose for the future."

It took a long time for Suzanne to work through her grief. Through it all, she grew closer to the Lord than ever and found new joy in walking with Him.

"Blessed are those who mourn, for they will be comforted." . . .

There is a time for everything, and a season for every activity under heaven: a time to be born and a time to die. . .a time to weep and a time to laugh, a time to mourn and a time to dance. . . .

Those who sow in tears will reap with songs of joy. He who goes out weeping, carrying seed to sow, will return with songs of joy, carrying sheaves with him. . . .

Praise be to the God and Father of our Lord Jesus Christ, the Father of compassion and the God of all comfort, who comforts us in all our troubles, so that we can comfort those in any trouble with the comfort we ourselves have received from God.

MATTHEW 5:4; ECCLESIASTES 3:1–2, 4;
PSALM 126:5–6; 2 CORINTHIANS 1:3–4 NIV

Thank You for Walking Me Through

The loss of my loved one is almost too much to bear, Lord. Still, I thank You for walking me through my grief—one step at a time.

When I can't understand what is happening, You are there. You manage to buffer the pain I'm facing. Thank You for holding me up as I begin to sort it all out.

"The eternal God is a dwelling place,
And underneath are [His] everlasting arms."
DEUTERONOMY 33:27 NASB

When I strike out in anger, I'm grateful I can pour out my feelings to You. Thank You for having such broad shoulders, Lord. Thank You for understanding my frustrations.

[Jesus said,] "Peace I leave with you, My peace I give to
you; not as the world gives do I give to you. Let not your
heart be troubled, neither let it be afraid."
JOHN 14:27 NKJV

When I frantically search for a way out of this devastating loss and do all I can to make things go the right way, I praise You for direction and strength.

Why are you downcast, O my soul?
Why so disturbed within me?
Put your hope in God,
for I will yet praise him,
my Savior and my God.
PSALM 42:5–6 NIV

When I feel abandoned by others, when no one seems to understand, I praise You for loving me. When depression obscures my recognizing Your presence, I thank You for remaining near. Thank You for interceding and taking my needs to the heavenly Father.

The Spirit helps us in our weakness. We do not know
what we ought to pray for, but the Spirit himself inter-
cedes for us with groans that words cannot express.
ROMANS 8:26 NIV

When the reality of my loss sets in, You help me find a way to accept what is happening. Thank You for reaching out and taking my hand and leading me.

> *He leads me beside the still waters.*
> *He restores my soul.*
> PSALM 23:2–3 NKJV

When I finally lay my burdens at Your feet, You have a marvelous way of giving me hope. In spite of my loss, You bring me through. Thank You for giving me help for today and hope for tomorrow. In You, Lord, there is no such thing as hopelessness.

Thank You for giving me a vision of the wonderful plans You have for my future. I praise You for giving me a deep, inner joy and a life abundant and free!

> *[Jesus said,] "I have come that they may have life,*
> *and that they may have it more abundantly."*
> JOHN 10:10 NKJV

God's Invitation

Come unto Me, soul falling apart.
Come unto Me, and give Me your heart.
Bring unto Me your grief and your loss.
Let all your tears spill down at the cross.

Bring anger, confusion—fear and defeat.
Leave all of them with Me each time we meet.
I'll heal every heartache and wrap you in love
Then fill you with comfort and peace from above.

ANITA CORRINE DONIHUE

A Third Birthday

Like many of us, I have lost family members and close friends through death. Although losing them leaves a huge void, God has comforted and healed me. Through Him, I've rediscovered my adventurous zeal for life after it had faded to almost nothing.

Now, I have a new love for this life God gives me. I get a kick out of little things, like watching one of our neighbor girls push her scooter down the street, her dark curly hair flying in the breeze. I love hearing the birds sing, watching the sun set, and the cat and squirrel chasing each other around the tree in our front yard. I love the laugh of a child when he (or she) tells a funny joke. I love it more when the only person who gets the joke is the child who tells it!

I love mountains and sunsets and March's unpredictable weather. I love the sweet-smelling summer nights when Bob and I sit on the patio and watch the first star come out.

But what I enjoy most is birthdays. They're celebrations of life. My calendar is filled with people's names and ages. I like to let people know I'm glad they are a part of my life and how special they are to me.

When my kids' birthdays roll around, I often think of their first cry and what they looked and felt like when I held them in my arms.

Three kinds of birthdays are most important to me. The first is the moment I was born. I'm sure I had no idea what was happening when I was thrust into this big, uncertain world. My wails of protest most likely made it clear how I felt at the time. I certainly don't recall. But God does. I like to imagine that upon my arrival He gathered me up in His arms and welcomed me into my new home here on earth.

My second birthday took place at the age of seven when I asked Jesus to come into my heart. It happened at a Good News Club meeting. The teacher carefully explained to me what it meant to be "born again." It didn't seem like a big deal—so simple to invite Him into my life. Something was happening, though. Unbeknownst to me, Jesus once again wrapped me in His arms and welcomed me as His child for eternity. His Spirit began to stir within my heart. Already, He started to help me with challenges I had to face in my young life. From the start, he was putting His plans into motion for my future.

I'm going to celebrate a third birthday someday. I'll shed this earthly body with all its inadequacies and receive a new one, along with a heavenly life with my Lord. Again, He will wrap His loving arms around me and welcome me to my new home.

I'm learning something about this third birthday. I bring to remembrance the stories my loved ones told me about their second birth when they received Christ. What about the third birthday? On the anniversary of my loved ones passing away, I think of their third and most wonderful birthday—one of finally enjoying a life that's full and free in heaven with the holy Tri-une—God the Father, God the Son, and God the Holy Spirit. What a time for celebration!

Let thy loving kindness, O Jehovah, be upon us,
For our heart shall rejoice in him,
According as we have hoped in thee.
Because we have trusted in his holy name.
PSALM 33:21–22 ASV

I will greatly rejoice in Jehovah, my soul shall be joyful in my God; for he hath clothed me with the garments of salvation, he hath covered me with the robe of righteousness, as a bridegroom decketh himself with a garland, and as a bride adorneth herself with her jewels.
ISAIAH 61:10 ASV

The righteous shall be glad in Jehovah, and shall take refuge in him; And all the upright in heart shall [praise him].
PSALM 64:10 ASV

Amazing Grace

'Twas grace that taught my heart to fear,
And grace my fears relieved;
How precious did that grace appear
The hour I first believed.

Through many dangers, toils, and snares,
I have already come;
'Tis grace hath brought me safe thus far,
And grace will lead me home.

When we've been there ten thousand years,
Bright shining as the sun,
We've no less days to sing God's praise
Than when we'd first begun.
JOHN NEWTON, 1725–1807

Earth recedes and Heaven opens. . . .
This is my coronation.
DWIGHT L. MOODY, 1837–1899

—It's a God-filled process!

BECOMING BEAUTIFUL

Kamryn Rose

My eight-year-old granddaughter, Kamryn Rose (better known as Kammy), is poetry in motion. She runs like a deer with her fiery auburn hair flying in the wind. She dives for the monkey bars in her family's yard and performs gravity-defying flips with total ease. How does this graceful little whirlwind manage to do that? I marvel every time I watch.

Kammy's family lives in the country, where there are more animals—domestic and wild—than people. She possesses an amazing ability to name each plant, tree, edible and nonedible berry, and every single animal. A soft side of her personality shows in the way she loves nature. She understands the habits of little and big creatures. She and her sister, Talia, take delight in helping a neighbor feed and care for three young steers.

Her creative talents shine in her growing cooking skills. She has fun adding an extra flair to whatever is being prepared for dinner. After the meal, Kammy often dances around the dining and living rooms, dressed in blues, lavenders, and purples. Her clear voice rings out the latest songs she has mastered. When evening comes, she loves to curl up with a good book. I can almost see her imagination soar high above rainbows and clouds as she reads to me and I to her.

Kammy has given herself the important job of adding merriment to everyone around her. Her cheerful disposition shines like the sun. Not long ago, I received a valentine from Kammy. Colorful stickers surrounded a lovely picture of Jesus. Inside was a message: "I love you, Nana."

What makes Kammy most beautiful is her sweet, pure love for Jesus. Not only is she pretty on the outside, but lovely on the inside, as well. She reminds me of a climber rose we have in our backyard called Joseph's Coat. Each spring, rosebuds burst forth in yellow, orange, white, pink, and red. I call it my Kamryn Rose.

Rose of Sharon

When Bob and I first purchased our "Kamryn Rose" bush, it looked like an unattractive stick. This didn't discourage us. The picture attached to the bush helped us visualize what the little twig would grow into. We carefully placed it in the ground and followed all the directions on how to care for it. It took awhile for the stick to develop into a green, leafy rosebush. But it finally did. Now the bush grows taller and fuller than all the other rosebushes in our garden.

I always thrill at the first sign of spring when new growth pops out on our rosebushes. As I feed and nurture them, I can almost see their branches stretch toward the spring rains. Buds form. The sun warms them. Finally, the blossoms open and show off a beauty that can come only from the Creator. Red velvets, silky pinks, cheerful shades of yellow, soft lavender, and (of course) the many colors of the Kamryn Rose bush. The fragrant blossoms of our rosebushes last from spring on into fall.

These roses cause me to think of Jesus. He is known as the Rose of Sharon, the Lily of the Valley, the Bright and Morning Star. He's the Alpha and Omega—the Beginning and the End. Sometimes when I tend our roses, I'm pricked by a thorn. Such a small irritation when compared to the crown of thorns Jesus wore for His crucifixion. He sacrificed His life so we can be free from sin and hopelessness. When we accept Him as our Savior, He provides us with a spiritual birth and a brand-new, exciting beginning with Him.

As we embark on our new lives with Jesus, we may not look like anything but a plain, ugly stick. Do we even show any promise of being a blessing to others? Yet Jesus has a picture of what *He* sees in us. We cannot grow on our own. We grow only as He tenderly showers us with His love. He softens and warms our hearts. He tends to our needs and feeds our souls. Our spirits lean toward His Spirit. We bask in His presence. Oh, how good it feels to be close to Him.

Some of our growth, however, may be slow and painful as Jesus prunes and trains us to yield to Him. But after awhile, the buds of our lives slowly develop through the work of His Holy Spirit. They pop open and display the beauty He has seen in us all along: Reds of love. Oranges of joy. Blues of peace. Greens of forgiveness and empathy. Pinks of kindness. Yellows of goodness. Purples of faithfulness. Lavenders of gentleness. And a rainbow full of self-control.

The more Jesus works in our lives, the more beautiful we become for Him. In no way do we take credit. Like the rose, our beauty comes only from the One who created us.

Behold the Beauty

Bonnie* finished her quick shower and slipped into her robe. She gazed into the mirror at her tired-looking reflection and forced herself to smile.

Bonnie has four children, ages two to twelve. Her part-time job and caring for her family keep her hopping to the point where she often feels exhausted. Yet she wouldn't change her life. She adores her husband and children, and cherishes the times they can spend together.

It was almost time for the kids to leave for school and for Bonnie to go to her part-time job. She quickly combed her hair and put on her makeup. Automatically, she tried to cover the dark shadows under her eyes. She thought of the lovely young girl she used to be. Was she still pretty? Maybe, but in a different way.

"Lord, I want to be beautiful in Your eyes. I want my husband and children to be proud of me." She sighed.

She immediately felt God's presence. There in her bathroom, He helped her see that she is the reflection of Him. He reminded her of how she loves her family and friends. Then He assured her that she really is beautiful both inside and out.

Bonnie glanced in the mirror for a final inspection before heading out the bathroom door. This time she saw a different woman—a woman of character and genuine loveliness. Her smile in the mirror was one of sincerity.

"Thank You, Lord. Through You, I *do* feel beautiful."

*Name changed.

An Honorable Woman

An excellent wife, who can find?
For her worth is far above jewels.
The heart of her husband trusts in her,
And he will have no lack of gain.
She does him good and not evil
All the days of her life.
She looks for wool and flax
And works with her hands in delight.
She is like merchant ships;
She brings her food from afar.
She rises also while it is still night
And gives food to her household
And portions to her maidens.
She considers a field and buys it;
From her earnings she plants a vineyard.
She girds herself with strength
And makes her arms strong.
She senses that her gain is good;
Her lamp does not go out at night.
She stretches out her hands to the distaff,
And her hands grasp the spindle.
She extends her hand to the poor,
And she stretches out her hands to the needy.
She is not afraid of the snow for her household,
For all her household are clothed with scarlet.

She makes coverings for herself;
Her clothing is fine linen and purple.
Her husband is known in the gates,
When he sits among the elders of the land.
She makes linen garments and sells them,
And supplies belts to the tradesmen.
Strength and dignity are her clothing,
And she smiles at the future.
She opens her mouth in wisdom,
And the teaching of kindness is on her tongue.
She looks well to the ways of her household,
And does not eat the bread of idleness.
Her children rise up and bless her;
Her husband also, and he praises her, saying:
"Many daughters have done nobly,
But you excel them all."
Charm is deceitful and beauty is vain,
But a woman who fears the LORD,
      she shall be praised.
Give her the product of her hands,
And let her works praise her in the gates.

PROVERBS 31:10–31 NASB

Who Am I, Lord?

Lord, my entire life is wrapped up in my husband and children, my church, and my job. Our kitchen calendar looks like a little bird walked across it with tracks going every direction at once. Sometimes we have two or three activities on the same night. Science-fair projects, track meets, ball games, concerts—the list goes on. Then there are the last-minute things, like a costume to be made for a play I wasn't told about. The church is my greatest love. Yet I often feel I'm rushing through the front door of this wonderful place of worship in my roller skates!

And, Lord, I want to tell You about my work. (I'm sure You already know.) Although it keeps me busy juggling responsibilities, I really enjoy my job. I like to put pride in what I do. When I complete a project, I feel good about a job well done.

Somewhere in all this commotion of children, church, and work, my husband and I manage to set aside time for each other. Funny how even when just the two of us go to the grocery store, it feels like we're out on a date. Thank You for the way our love grows more every year.

I'm grateful for all these things, Lord. But who am I? I know I'm a wife, a mother, a church leader, and an employee. But who am I deep down inside? My life revolves so much around others that I'm not sure where I fit in as a person.

You know me better than anyone. Please help me with this. Although I'm older and don't look as young as I used to, am I still beautiful? I had dreams and goals when I was younger. Is it all right to still have dreams and goals in this stage of my life?

In the midst of all our activities, help me to find time for myself. Show me, I pray, how to understand who I am. Reveal to me the personal worth and beauty You see.

My little child, your loveliness comes from deep within your soul. It is shown by the purity and reverence you have for Me. It isn't found in fine clothing, lovely hair, or expensive jewelry. Instead, it comes from deep within your inner self. As you reflect Me, I give you a loving spirit and a beauty that shall never fade.

You are of great worth to Me, dear child. As you put your hope in Me and seek to follow My ways, the more beautiful you will become. The more you love Me, the more you will learn to love and appreciate yourself. Your talents, the work you do, the care you give to others—all these things make you the treasured person you are.

As you grow older, your beauty won't fade. Those around you will see the graciousness of a fine Christian who loves Me. Always remember, I do not look upon the surface of your appearance. I look deep within your heart.

Remain close to Me and listen intently to My direction. In so doing, I will give you goals and dreams. I will give you hope and blessings beyond measure. I do this because you are My lovely, dear child; and you belong to Me.

When I look into the eyes of my child,
I know he or she depends on me.
When I look into the eyes of my child,
I feel the responsibility.
When I look into the eyes of my child,
I understand why *God loves me.*
ROBERT DONIHUE SR., 2006

Stepping in the Light

Trying to walk in the steps of the Savior,
Trying to follow our Savior and King,
Shaping our lives by His blessed example,
Happy, how happy, the songs that we bring.

Walking in footsteps of gentle forbearance,
Footsteps of faithfulness, mercy, and love,
Looking to Him for the grace freely promised,
Happy, how happy, our journey above.

How beautiful to walk in the steps of our Savior,
Stepping in the light, stepping in the light;
How beautiful to walk in the steps of the Savior,
Led in paths of light.
        WILLIAM J. KIRKPATRICK, 1838–1921

Youth fades; love droops; the leaves of friendship fall.
A mother's secret love outlives them all.
OLIVER WENDELL HOLMES, 1809–1894

—It's a God-filled process!

PHYSICALLY FIT

An Ounce of Prevention

"An ounce of prevention is worth a pound of cure." Perhaps you've heard this age-old maxim. While I was growing up, my grandmother applied this saying to many aspects of my life: cleaning my room; being careful about what I said or did; and getting my homework completed on time. However, the application of this quote has stayed with me most in learning to take care of my health. Grandma lived what she preached by being careful about what she ate and getting plenty of exercise. She enjoyed a good, long life.

Bob and I have always enjoyed walking together. This habit began when we first met, and has continued for over forty-six years of marriage. When we started dating, we walked all over town. We wandered through shops, sometimes stopping for a root beer at the local XXX Root Beer Restaurant.

At the time, food really didn't enter our thoughts much. Yet now, food, especially junk food, is much more alluring. Resisting temptation has become a part of our nice, long walks. As we stroll along Main Street, we pass by the pizza shop, the local bakery, the fast-food restaurants, and the deli. The most tempting of all is the little store displaying the sign HOMEMADE FUDGE.

This is when the Lord reminds me to use self-control. Along with exercising physically, I'm learning to practice self-control in what I eat (or don't eat). "An ounce of prevention is worth a pound of cure," so I can enjoy many happy, healthy days with my friends and family, and serve the Lord.

Take Hold of Life

When we struggle with ailments, we often depend on God to restore our health. Along with placing our faith in Him, I believe God expects us to do all we can to help ourselves. He has given us doctors, medicine, and willpower on our part to get well. When we work hand in hand with the Great Physician, we experience His healing blessings.

The following story is about someone who did all of these things. She is a walking miracle.

Rosaura's Story

When I first became friends with Rosaura*, I was immediately impressed by how she enjoyed life to the fullest. She loved the Lord and was active in church. She taught Spanish to groups of eager students in school. Along with serving the Lord and helping others, Rosaura and her husband, Phil, took pleasure in going to musicals and plays. For outdoor sports, they often enjoyed rock climbing and long-distance running. Then about three years ago, tragedy changed her life.

Rosaura's ears plugged up, and she became dizzy. When she went to the doctor, he prescribed a nasal spray. The medicine didn't help.

A few weeks later, she began having pain in her left arm. The doctor told her at times this would happen. He didn't explain why but said to keep using the nasal spray. The pain worsened, so Rosaura stopped using the atomizer. A month passed. Although the pain left her arm, dizziness persisted. Doctors prescribed different medicines. Nothing helped.

Rosaura and Phil realized she was facing serious problems. Her heart palpitated. Her hands grew clammy. She often felt light-headed. She experienced continual motion sickness. She couldn't sleep at night. When she struggled out of bed, she had to lean against a wall to gain her balance.

Rosaura and Phil united in prayer for her healing. Their family, church congregation, and Christian friends joined them in prayer. In spite of her misery, she was determined to remain active. One day while running a 10K with Phil, she became so dizzy she almost fainted. She had no choice but to stop running until her health returned.

Specialists were called in. Rosaura underwent a multitude of tests. Doctors checked her for allergies and recommended changes in her diet. Still, nothing helped. Her condition gradually worsened until she was barely able to stand. Blood tests showed an extremely low platelet count. There was a risk that her blood would not clot properly. Doctors said antibodies were attacking her platelets.

Her muscles cramped with painful spasms. Controlling her unsteady body took all her energy. Doctors told her that anxiety made digestion difficult. Her weight plummeted to just over one hundred pounds. She was losing muscle mass. She developed a painful case of shingles, which the doctors also attributed to high anxiety and stress. Her active world was shrinking. At times, the only place she felt all right was in her bed, curled up in a little ball. She wondered if she was losing her mind.

More than ever, Rosaura called on the Lord for help. This time she asked Him to fight this battle for her. "What's happening to me, Lord?" she cried. "I'm getting so tired. Heal me, I pray!"

Day after day, she sang praises to the Lord at the top of her lungs. "My God is an awesome God!" Each time she sang, she felt God's calming presence.

Rosaura's condition worsened, and she had trouble teaching. Panic repeatedly rushed over her. She couldn't go into crowded places. Rosaura remained in the car and talked with her husband on a walkie-talkie when they shopped. She became fearful of even her own classroom and cut back to teaching two hours a day. Occasionally she couldn't teach at all.

In spite of her struggles, she kept attending church, sitting in the narthex. Each time she became fearful, she squeezed Phil's hand. Some people discouraged her, saying she would never get well. Others assumed she didn't have enough faith, or she must have had some hatred in her life and God was punishing her. Some avoided her, perhaps not knowing what to say. Others assured her of their love and prayers and told her that God would see her through.

Odors triggered panic attacks. Her heart palpitations and chest pain worsened. She wondered if she was having a heart attack. Would she die?

Rosaura grew so weak she could barely crawl out of bed. Tears rolled down her cheeks as she prayed, "Lord, what's wrong with me? Help me! Help the doctors. Heal me. I can't take this any longer."

When she had the strength to read her Bible, Rosaura found comfort and peace beyond anything she had experienced before. She thought of the time Jesus stilled the storm. *"And he arose, and rebuked the wind, and said unto the sea, Peace, be still. And the wind ceased, and there was a great calm"* (MARK 4:39 KJV).

Over and over, she read a prayer from *When I'm on My Knees*, entitled "Singing in the Storms." She knew He would cause *her* storm to also pass.

Because her platelets kept going up and down, the doctors recommended a bone marrow biopsy. Before the procedure, Rosaura was advised to make out a will. She was terribly afraid. But she was determined to rely on God.

The biopsy was clear. Rosaura rejoiced. She didn't have cancer! Her prayers for healing changed to prayers of praise and thanksgiving. She constantly felt His presence surround and fill her.

"Lord, *You* are with me. Lord, You *are* with me!" She knew God was bringing her through this, and she would be victorious.

After a three-year struggle, Rosaura was diagnosed with acute anxiety disorder caused by an imbalance of the brain chemical serotonin. Through proper medication, a high-protein diet, counseling, and lots of prayer and determination, Rosaura reclaimed her life, one step at a time. Writing in her prayer journal helped a lot, and she began to walk and talk with the Lord each day.

She's running and rock climbing again. She's back to teaching full time. Rosaura feels she can empathize with her students when they struggle, because of her own struggles.

What helped Rosaura's recovery most was going to the Lord in prayer, reading the Bible and good Christian books, and taking the proper medication. One prayer she continues to read is entitled "I Will Never Give Up." Through it all, Rosaura's relationship with the Lord has grown tremendously. He is her dearest friend. She treasures life, and she treasures her health. She has learned how to pace her activities, listen to her body, and be reasonable about the expectations she puts on herself. She feels life is too short to worry or complain about little things. God has used this experience to bless her and make her faith in Him stronger. She's more patient with those around her. She's learning to tune in, reach out, and love other people in their times of need with prayer, a card, a visit, or a phone call.

Rosaura says, "You may go through hard times. But with the Lord, you can move forward. Don't ever give up!"

*Written with permission from Rosaura Milliman.

But now the Lord who created you, O Israel, says, Don't be afraid, for I have ransomed you; I have called you by name; you are mine. When you go through deep waters and great trouble, I will be with you. When you go through rivers of difficulty, you will not drown! When you walk through the fire of oppression, you will not be burned up—the flames will not consume you. For I am the Lord your God, your Savior, the Holy One of Israel.
ISAIAH 43:1–3 TLB

God does far more than just Band-Aids on our hurts. He is the ultimate Healer.

I Will Never Give Up

Lord, right now I feel helpless and alone. There appears to be no hope. Please, show me You are near. People say my situation is a lost cause. Yet Your infinite wisdom and mercy continue to prove that You are near, helping me along the way, showing Your will. Even in troubled times my voice breaks out in song, praising You for Your power and forgiving mercy. No, I will never give up but seek You out, day by day, hour by hour.

How many times have I disappointed You and pleaded for Your forgiveness? Your eternal love forgives me over and over.

When troubles surround me, I will not be afraid. In the midst of hopelessness, I feel Your helping hand. In spite of my failings, I know Your compassion and forgiveness. In the midst of my broken pride, I sense Your strength and comfort. In my loss of direction, I look to Your leading.

I thank You, already, for how You lift me from the depths of despair, how You help and heal, how You forgive and offer favor to last me all of my life.

I will always be secure in Your protection. I won't be shaken. I will stand steadfast and sure. *I will never give up.* Thanks be to You, O Lord.

*Taken from *When I'm on My Knees.*

So take a new grip with your tired hands, stand firm on your shaky legs, and mark out a straight, smooth path for your feet so that those who follow you, though weak and lame, will not fall and hurt themselves, but become strong.
HEBREWS 12:12–13 TLB

Your Healing Hands

When illness strikes its brutal blow
With pain beyond degree,
I often feel like giving up,
Still, I will lean on Thee.

My temples throb, my muscles cramp,
From fever's vise-like hold,
Yet in the midst of suffering,
Your presence, I behold.

O Great Physician, so divine,
How good to have You near.
I feel Your soothing hands on me,
My drooping heart, You cheer.

Take now my aches and pains, dear Lord,
I place my trust in Thee.
Anoint me with Your healing balm.
In You, I am set free.

The Great Physician

The Great Physician now is near,
The sympathizing Jesus;
He speaks the drooping heart to cheer,
Oh, hear the voice of Jesus.

WILLIAM HUNTER, 1811–1877

The Best Medicine

When we ask ourselves how we can stay physically fit, a list of goals most likely comes to mind:

1. Eat properly, and take vitamins.
2. Get an adequate amount of rest.
3. Take time to exercise.
4. Get regular checkups from doctors.
5. Take medicine when prescribed.

All of these things are good. But there's a different kind of medicine that's necessary for our well-being. It's the medicine of a cheerful heart.

The Bible tells us, "A cheerful heart does good like medicine, but a broken spirit makes one sick" (Proverbs 17:22 TLB), and "The joy of the Lord is your strength. You must not be dejected and sad!" (Nehemiah 8:10 TLB).

These lessons on being cheerful are proven true by

today's medical studies. Good old-fashioned belly laughs from deep down inside cause us to breathe deeply. When we enjoy a good laugh, it releases adrenaline and supplies additional oxygen to our bodies and brains. It makes us more alert, sends out natural pain killers, loosens the knots in our necks, reduces stress, and helps improve relationships. A good belly laugh is as beneficial as working out on exercise equipment (and a whole lot easier). Along with easing tension, laughing helps burn calories.

Let's remind ourselves throughout the day to not dwell on the negative, but to think positively and look at things on the bright side: "For as he thinks in his heart, so is he" (Proverbs 23:7 NKJV). Let's curl up our face muscles, make a smile, and pass it on. Chances are we'll get some smiles back. Medical research shows that when we smile, our facial muscles tell our brain to think more positively. When we do this, it triggers our entire being to feel better.

Remember, there is always hope. No matter what the situation, we can find hope in the Lord Jesus Christ.

Joy Unspeakable

I have found the joy no tongue can tell,
How its waves of glory roll!
It is like a great o'erflowing well,
Springing up within my soul.
BARNEY ELLIOTT WARREN, 1867–1951

A glad outlook each day keeps the gloom away.
—It's a God-filled process!

FAITHFUL FRIENDS

Blessings Because of Faithfulness

Mixed feelings of excitement and anxiousness may have stirred within Abram's heart when the Lord God called him to leave his country in Haran and move to the land of Canaan. Leaving his father, his long-cherished friendships from childhood, and his special memories had to be painful.

Without hesitation, Abram submitted to God's call. He left his country, a land of graven images. Even his father and other family members had become idolaters. Abram obediently broke away and made a new life for his household and his nephew, Lot.

He had no idea where God was leading him or what lay ahead in the land of Canaan. But Abram did know one thing. God had promised He would always be with Abram and would bless him and his descendants in years to come.

Sometime later, Abram, Sarai, and their household, along with Lot and his household, settled between Bethel and Ai. God blessed them so that their flocks and herds multiplied abundantly—to the point where there wasn't room for the two households. Discord grew between them.

Abram generously offered Lot his choice of land. Lot chose the plain of Jordon near the city of Sodom, where there were meadows with rich soil and plenty of water. Such fertile country appeared to be a good choice. Lot was a just man. Sadly, people in Sodom lived terribly wicked lives. The city's environment was not a decent setting for anyone. Lot's decision to live there would bring much grief upon him and Abram.

Abram moved his household to Mamre. The land was mountainous and rocky, unlike the fertile valley Lot had chosen. Abram had a different reason than Lot for making his choice. This was the land God led him to. By faith, Abram lived in the promised land even though it was foreign to him. He and his family dwelled in tents instead of houses. Their tent city had been built on a strong spiritual foundation. The builder was the Lord God.

The Lord promised Abram another blessing. He told him to look to the north, the south, the east, and the west. All of it would be given to Abram and his descendants. The number of his offspring would be incalculable, like the dust of the earth.

Unfortunately, things didn't remain calm for Abram and his family. A turn of events forced this kindhearted man to become a warrior. A fierce conflict broke out in the valley among the different kings.

A multitude of captives were taken and treasured belongings, stolen. Right in the middle of it all dwelled Lot. Sure enough, Lot and his household were carried off, along with all of Lot's possessions.

In spite of Lot's foolish choice of ignoring righteous living and putting himself outside God's protection, Abram loved his nephew enough to come to his rescue. Abram's emotions probably peaked with concern and determination when he rounded up all 318 of his faithful, trained young servants. In the middle of the night, they stormed into the valley and surrounded the enemy camp. In a flash, they overthrew the adversaries and had them on the run. Abram and his servants recovered all the loot and rescued Lot and his people.

Overwhelming victory for Abram in this battle may well have convinced the kings that God was watching over Abram and his family. Perhaps this struck a chord of fear and respect. A victory, indeed. Yet the next battle Abram faced was far more subtle.

Abram could have fallen into greed at this point. Instead, it is speculated, he gave one-tenth of the recovered loot to Melchizedek, the high priest. Perhaps Abram planned to return belongings to the king of Sodom, as well. But the king of Sodom made Abram an offer that was filled with wrong. The king wanted every person he had once captured to be returned to him, and he promised all the spoils would go to Abram.

Abram would have no part of such a scheme. No way would he compromise his standards and accept gifts from a pagan leader. In Genesis 14:22–23, we read: "Abram said to the king of Sodom, 'I have sworn to the LORD God Most High, possessor of heaven and earth, that I will not take a thread or a sandal thong or anything that is yours, for fear you would say, "I have made Abram rich"'"(NASB).

Because Abram obeyed God, he was blessed. God caused his descendants to multiply "as the stars of the heavens and as the sand which is on the seashore" (Genesis 22:17 NASB). No longer would his name be Abram. Instead, his name rang down through history as Abraham, father of many nations.

God, Give Us Friends

God, give us friends with whom to share
Our joys, our aims, our cares, our strife;
May loyal lives in fruitage bear,
The deeper fellowship of life.

God, give us friends for whom we hear
The Master's call to love and lift;
In service true, with hearts sincere,
May we spend "Love," God's holy gift.

May friendship prove a sacred trust,
A heav'nly gift of priceless worth;
A link to bind our hearts to God,
Through "Love Divine" reborn on earth.

FLORENCE ANGELA BOYCE,
EIGHTEENTH-CENTURY WRITER

Bless Our Friendships

Thank You for my loyal friend, Lord. She's always willing to take a few moments just to talk—and listen. We each often understand how the other feels. I'm grateful for when we got to spend an evening together in her home. In spite of our busy schedules, we shared a meal. Afterward, we settled into our chairs and enjoyed catching up on all that was happening.

Another night, the phone rang. My friend from out of state called. What a bond we shared across the miles! She told me of some heartaches her family was going through. We talked for an hour and prayed together.

You provide valuable components in these friendships, Lord. One is the way we keep loving and caring for each other through the thick and thin of our lives. Another is that we share a common tie of truly loving You. Most precious is how we can unite in prayer for each other's concerns.

Thank You for these faithful friends, Lord. They are few. But they are ones who stick closer to me than a brother or sister. Through life, may our friendships always remain.

But friendship is the breathing rose,
with sweets in every fold.
OLIVER WENDELL HOLMES, 1809–1894

A true friend is always loyal. . . .
There are "friends" who pretend to be friends, but there
is a friend who sticks closer than a brother [or sister].
PROVERBS 17:17; 18:24 TLB

I Would Be True

I would be true, for there are those who trust me;
I would be pure, for there are those who care;
I would be strong, for there is much to suffer;
I would be brave, for there is much to dare.
I would be brave, for there is much to dare.

I would be friend of all—the foe, the friendless;
I would be giving, and forget the gift;
I would be humble, for I know my weakness;
I would look up, and laugh, and love, and lift;
I would look up, and laugh, and love, and lift.
Amen.

HOWARD ARNOLD WALTER, 1883–1918

Oh, the blessings from God, which come full
  circle to the faithful with willing hearts.
        —It's a God-filled process!

Triumph over Temptation

Switching Grips

It was a crisp October morning when Eric joined his father-in-law, Aaron, in Carnation, Washington. He was looking forward to a great day of fly-fishing. Eric, fishing instructor Aaron, students, and friends gathered at the Tolt River, just above where it pours into the Snoqualmie.

Eric chose his fishing spot a little way downstream from the group. He glanced around at the beauty of God's creation. He took a deep breath. Nature's peace and tranquility made it easy to daydream a bit. He shrugged into his chest-high waders and coat. The waders were a little big, but he felt confident they would keep him dry. Eric reorganized his gear and grabbed the rod he had borrowed from his father-in-law. Then he eased his way into the water and cast out his line. There had been a lot of rain that fall, so the Tolt River was pretty high.

Instead of staying close to shore, Eric worked his way out toward the middle of the river. He let his line drift downstream. Eric's main focus was to catch fish.

He was so preoccupied, he didn't notice how far out he had waded or the deepening currents swirling past him. He was startled to discover the water had almost reached his waist. It was too deep to be safe! He had to get closer to shore as quickly as possible. All at once, the rock he stood on shifted. Eric lost his footing and fell into the icy river. The strong current began to whisk him downstream. Water immediately gushed into his waders. A shiver jolted his entire body. Thankfully, his waders were constructed to keep him afloat even when filled with water. He paddled desperately but was unable to get out of his situation.

"Help!" he shouted.

No one seemed to hear his frantic cry.

The rushing river pushed Eric along fifty or sixty more feet. The swift drag sucked him toward a steep bank lined with blackberry bushes. He lunged at the plants and missed. After several attempts, he grasped a strong blackberry vine with one bare hand. It wasn't enough. He needed both hands, so he let go of Aaron's rod and clung to the vines. Again, Eric shouted for help. Again, no one could hear his cries above the river's roar.

The current continued to rage mercilessly past his chest and into his waders, trying to drag him under.

The pull of the water was more than his waders could handle. He clung to the blackberry vines with all his strength. If he let go, he would be swept away. He felt his only hope was in the strength of the vines.

At that moment, Eric remembered he could call on Someone who was always close enough to hear. It was the Lord. He was Eric's best friend. "God, help me," he pleaded through clenched teeth.

Upstream, Aaron and his group heard a noise. They thought it was a dog barking. The noise persisted.

"It's Eric!" Someone finally realized.

The group hurried along the road, following the sounds of Eric's shouts for help. When they spotted him, they slid down the bank and into the bushes where he clung to the blackberry vines.

By now, Eric's hands were torn and bloody. He felt someone reaching for him. But he was afraid to let go of the blackberry bushes. His father-in-law grabbed his wrist. Another took hold of him. Then another. Eric had to let go and allow his friends to pull him to safety. He released his grip on the thorny vines and grabbed hold of his rescuers. It was then they were able to lift him from the river. Later, Eric noticed his hurting, bleeding hands.

He was amazed that he had refused to let go of the thorns tearing into his flesh in exchange for the hands that were rescuing him.

Eric and Aaron still enjoy fishing in the Tolt River. Eric continues to wear his chest-high waders. But he never allows the water to go above his knees. He acknowledges how unpredictable and treacherous rivers can be. Now he stays alert to his surroundings and heeds important safety measures.

He continues to thank God for using his father-in-law and friends to pull him to safety that day. Still, he knows there were two more hands that rescued him. They were the hands of God.

*Written with permission from Eric Kilbury.

A Sure Grasp

Like Eric, do you ever go along without being wary of the temptations and dangers around you? When life becomes comfortable, do you become distracted from the things of the Lord and neglect the wonderful times you and God can enjoy together? Because of your distractions and lack of time with the Lord, do you sometimes feel lured into things that aren't pleasing to Him? Are you shocked at how unpredictable and treacherous choices outside of His will can be? Perhaps before you know it, you've been caught up in a current of confusion and sucked into disasters far too difficult to get out of on your own.

Have you ever been unable to turn away from poor choices? Or sought advice and help from the wrong people? Have the results dragged you down to despair? In order to survive, have you become too fearful to let go of wrong things and the people who caused you difficulty and hurt you the most?

No matter how much trouble you find yourself in, it's never too late to cry out to God. He's only a prayer away. He hears you over the roar of life's treacherous "rivers." Like Eric's reluctance to let go of the thorny bushes, don't be afraid to let go of the things that are hurting you. Switch your grip from false-blackberry-bush-type hopes to your heavenly Father's sure grasp.

You'll be surprised at the way He will whisper words of encouragement and direction to your heart. He will use circumstances to work things together for your good in amazing ways. He will be your Guide. As you search in the Bible, He'll provide answers that are certain and true. Purpose in your heart and mind to live a new life, pleasing and holy to Him. No longer will you need to function under uncertain and danger-ous circumstances. Instead, God will help you triumph over them. Each time you call on Him, He'll provide an escape and help keep you from being sucked into such things. Grasp His hand. Tenderly yet firmly God will set your feet on a sturdy path—a path where He will bless your heart and mind with assurance and peace.

Rise Above

Father, I'm facing some difficult times right now. They happened before I even knew what was coming. Although I'm tempted to compromise the standards You've set for me, I pray that Your staying grace will help me do what's right in Your eyes. Let me think on You, rather than making wrong choices that could only lead to more trouble.

When I'm ridiculed and belittled for following You, I pray for graciousness. Help me not to lash out and stomp away with a negative attitude. Father, keep me from having a false holier-than-thou pride. Instead, let me rise above the circumstances. When things get tough, remind me to pray for those who are mistreating me. Teach me to be a living example of You in everything I say and do.

Grant me the discernment to be sensitive to the needs of those I'm praying for and to put into practice the scripture in Proverbs 25:21–22: "If your enemy is hungry, give him food! If he is thirsty, give him something to drink! This will make him feel ashamed of himself, and God will reward you" (TLB). Help me to do these things with a pure heart, with a genuine love for the other person, not seeking a means to get my own way.

I read in the Bible that there are no temptations or trials I face that others haven't already gone through. You were tempted, Lord. And You overcame temptation! The same Spirit who empowered You during those times of temptation is here within me today.

Thank You for making ways of escape so I won't be faced with too much to bear. I wish I could be joyful when I'm faced with trials. Still, I thank You for helping my faith in You to grow, and for teaching me how to become more patient. Along with my learning to be patient, grant me the strength to stand up for what is right in Your eyes. Lord, I pray for You to create a refined work in me. I want You to fulfill in me the purpose You have in the whole scheme of things.

Thank You for assuring me with Your love and comfort as I endure temptations and trials. Thank You for taking the burdens from me and working them out according to Your will. *As my hand grasps Yours, I'm grateful You help me rise above each situation.* I praise You for giving me a sense of well-being and confidence—a confidence that in You I live and move and have my being. For You are in me, and I am in You.

The harvest of happiness is reaped
from seeds of kindness.

A Prayer

Lord, make me an instrument of Thy peace.
Where there is hatred, let me sow love.
Where there is injury, pardon.
Where there is doubt, faith.
Where there is despair, hope.
Where there is darkness, light.
Where there is sadness, joy.
SAINT FRANCIS OF ASSISI, 1181–1226

But remember this—the wrong desires that come into your life aren't anything new and different. Many others have faced exactly the same problems before you. And no temptation is irresistible. You can trust God to keep the temptation from becoming so strong that you can't stand up against it, for he has promised this and will do what he says. He will show you how to escape temptation's power so that you can bear up patiently against it.

1 CORINTHIANS 10:13 TLB

Victory

I am trusting in the Lord,
I am anchored on His Word,
Victory, victory.
I have peace and joy within,
Since my heart is free from sin,
Victory, victory.

Victory, yes, victory;
Hallelujah! I am free,
Jesus gives me victory!
Glory, glory hallelujah!
He is all in all to me.
BARNEY ELLIOTT WARREN, 1867–1951

God's Certainty

Look not for faith.
Look at God's faithfulness.
Look not to circumstance.
Look at God's certainty.

—It's a God-filled process!

REWARD IN THE RUBBLE

Divine Appointment

It was seven o'clock in the morning when Bob and I pulled into the Trailways Transit parking garage. I was leaving to spend a few days with our son and his family in northeastern Washington. Bob couldn't go along on this trip because of other commitments. Since I was traveling alone, I decided not to drive six hours over two mountain passes. I wanted to leave the driving to someone else. Taking the bus was a good option for me.

For some people, traveling by bus is inconvenient and uncomfortable. In spite of cramped muscles and lack of sleep, I often get caught up in the adventure of taking in the scenery and meeting people from all walks of life. The moment my feet step through the terminal doorway, I silently ask God to lead me to the person He wants me to encourage and talk with about Him. I didn't know that—this time—God would answer my prayer before I even climbed on the bus.

Bob and I prayed for my safety. We walked into the terminal, where I verified my tickets. We hugged and kissed good-bye. Then he was on his way to an important appointment. I shuffled my baggage through a maze of people and attempted to find a seat. There was an hour-long wait until boarding.

One young man, not more than twenty years old, glanced up at me. He scooted over and offered me a seat. I gratefully accepted. He sat quietly, looking straight ahead. His face showed etchings of character and hard work. He wore a white baseball cap and a sports jersey with the number 19 on it.

"Thank you for giving me a place to sit," I offered.

"You're welcome." He responded with no expression. Not even a smile.

Could this be the person God wanted me to minister to? I sent up my usual silent arrow prayer for guidance. Immediately, God answered.

"Where are you heading?" I ventured.

"Louisiana," he answered in broken English.

After a few minutes of visiting, I learned that his name was Berger.* He had moved from Kuwait to the United States with his parents, brother, and sister. They also lived in Louisiana.

I told him a little about my family and that I was a teacher. Then I listened.

Berger was returning to college in Louisiana after visiting for a few days with friends in the Seattle area. His face broke into a big smile.

"I'm about to get my degree in engineering," he said proudly. He went on to explain how his parents strongly encouraged him and his brother and sister to put all their efforts into what they worked toward. "God expects nothing less than my best. I thank Him every day for giving me the opportunity to have a good education."

Berger paused. He appeared to be deep in thought. He continued quietly—almost as though he were talking to himself. "One thing troubles me. I'm saddened when some people say they can't, for one reason or another."

He sighed. His voice grew more intent. He looked at me and held out his palms to emphasize his point. "They can! They can try. And try again. And when they do try like I do, they will surprise themselves at what they can accomplish—especially when they ask God for His help."

I explained how I, too, loved the Lord. We talked some more about dreams and goals and downright hard work.

Before I knew it, my bus arrived.

Without a second thought, I looked into Berger's eyes and spoke with sincerity. "No matter where you go, no matter what happens along the way, God will watch out for you."

We shook hands, exchanged a "God bless you," and went our separate ways.

After I climbed on the bus, I wondered why I had assured Berger of God's care with such authority. It certainly didn't come from me.

Were You leading me to say that, Lord?

Two days later, I read in the newspaper how Hurricane Katrina had torn its way through Louisiana. I wondered what Berger had found when he reached his destination. I bowed my head over the paper and asked God to help this young man. I prayed for Berger to be able to use his engineering skills and keep-trying attitude to help folks rebuild their homes and lives.

It was then that I realized God really did guide me to tell Berger: "No matter where you go, no matter what happens, God will watch out for you."

Where was the reward for Berger in this horrible Louisiana rubble? Perhaps it was a divine appointment, where he was reminded of God's love and care.

*Name changed.

A Greater Vision

The day for Pastor Don and Courtney Elbourne and their congregation began like any other, except for one thing. A hurricane was on the way. Some people in their area of Mississippi had weathered many hurricanes and knew how to prepare for them. But this storm was different.

Like a violent monster, Hurricane Katrina tore a deadly path through Lakeshore, Mississippi. There hadn't been one this bad since the 1800s. Everywhere it whipped, the forty-two-foot storm surge carelessly tossed houses, cars, and even large buildings as if they were plastic toys. Trees were jerked out by their roots and cast aside like unwanted toothpicks. Huge waves tore homes from their foundations and shoved them into the sea. Everything was reduced to rubble with splintered boards, smashed furniture, and downed power poles strewn as far as the eye could see. The beautiful Lakeshore Baptist Church building was gone. Water filled the city like a huge bathtub. Lakeshore was one of the areas hit hardest by Hurricane Katrina.

Every member of the church congregation survived the storm. They were thankful to be alive. Many folks were forced to evacuate their homes. It became impossible for them to return for weeks. Some had to wait for months. When they returned to their home sites, the destruction was unbelievable, their loss devastating. The few buildings standing were no longer safe to live in. The nearest hotel and hospital were an hour's drive away. The water wasn't safe to drink. No bathrooms. No stores or restaurants. No place to sleep.

Volunteers began mucking out houses, rebuilding, cooking, and sorting food and supplies. When people asked Pastor Don what they could bring to help, he replied, "A consistent relationship with Christ, a willingness to serve, and an attitude past flexibility—right into fluid."

Constant words of encouragement filled e-mail messages and cell phone lines. Folks from all over the United States flocked into Lakeshore to help. Workers began the rebuilding process of putting up tents, port-a-potties, and shower trailers. A tent sanctuary, a large hut, and a tent city were built. Somehow, God would help them make it through.

Where were God's blessings found in the midst of such tragedy? They were found when these people placed their faith in an unfailing God. The more they trusted God, the more He blessed them.

A Laundromat not far from the tent church survived the storm. Workers piped in water that couldn't be used for drinking and put the facility to good use. Even still, there's a sign on the door that says: Free Laundromat by Lakeshore Baptist Church.

People came to the church for assistance. Some who had never come before wanted to know why help was available to them. They were told: "God loves you."

Church attendance doubled. Souls were being reached for the Lord. Had it not been for Katrina's disaster, some may have never heard the gospel. Powerful and enthusiastic testimonies bubbled from local families and from volunteers who met in Bible study groups. They told everyone how God is in control and has a purpose, and that He is able to take suffering people and point them to the cross of Jesus.

God is still moving in a remarkable way in the rebuilding of Lakeshore. People from all walks of life, young and old, are uniting their efforts. Values are being changed. Material possessions have been replaced with God's eternal blessings.

When volunteers return home, their lives are often transformed. Petty problems aren't important anymore. Little things, like complaining about a cold hamburger or a flat tire, pale in light of the priceless lessons God has given them.

Pastor Don says, "There's a connection between Christianity and Katrina."

God is the blessing in the rubble. He really does work out all things for good for those who love and trust Him.

A Shelter in the Time of Storm

The Lord's our rock, in Him we hide,
A shelter in the time of storm;
Secure whatever ill betide,
A shelter in the time of storm.

O Rock divine, O Refuge dear,
A shelter in the time of storm;
Be Thou our Helper ever near,
A shelter in the time of storm.

WORDS BY VERNON J. CHARLESWORTH, 1839–1915
MUSIC BY IRA D. SANKEY, 1840–1908

LORD, I NEED YOUR BLESSING

Angels of Hope

Among many encouraging people at Lakeshore Baptist Church are Bea Everett and Violet Patterson. They spread sunshine wherever they go.

Those who talk with Bea by phone or in person enjoy the blessings she has to share. She tells everyone how God faithfully provides for the church's needs almost immediately after they pray. One time, the church was nearly out of paper towels and toilet paper. As usual, the congregation went to prayer. Within an hour the items were brought in by the truckload.

Violet is a widow. Her husband passed away a few years ago. The storm forced her to evacuate her home. All seemed futile. Plans were under way to bulldoze her house to the ground. Before the final decision was made, Violet took the matter to the Lord in prayer. She asked Him to "open a door." It took a lot of work, but her home was restored by faithful volunteers.

Bea and Violet are constantly praising God for His faithful blessings. There is no room in their lives for self-pity. Instead, the Lord blesses them with beautiful expressions that mirror His love. Their contagious smiles spread cheer to everyone they meet.

Truly, God has made them angels of hope.

A happy heart makes the face cheerful,
but heartache crushes the spirit.
PROVERBS 15:13 NIV

Let kindness come with every gift,
and good desires with every greeting.
ROBERT LOUIS STEVENSON, 1850–1894

Hidden Treasure

Have you ever faced situations so difficult that the outcome appeared hopeless? During those times, did you know that the person you could count on to bring you through was the Lord? In the midst of everything, did you find yourself asking God to show you one good thing to keep you going? I know I have.

Although folks at Lakeshore Baptist Church were being blessed with volunteers from all over, God must have known they needed a sign from Him. Amazingly, it showed up like hidden treasure.

One day (not long after Katrina) a man was walking in the woods. He came upon something white that was sticking up from the rubble. To his surprise, he found a church steeple completely intact! It turned out to be the steeple from the Lakeshore Baptist Church building.

Volunteers hauled the steeple to the church site and erected it as a declaration of hope. By then, the tent sanctuary had been replaced by a long metal building. Today when folks drive down the road toward the church, they can see a steeple shining above the surrounding devastation. A sign on it reads:

LAKESHORE BAPTIST CHURCH
6028 LAKE SHORE ROAD
PASTOR DON ELBOURNE

God gave the church and community a visible reminder of His constant love and care during difficult times. This once-hidden treasure symbolizes something far more valuable than buildings and belongings. Pastor Don's wife, Courtney, reminds the congregation that their treasure lies in showing kindness to others. It's about true giving from the depths of their hearts. What little they have, they have learned to share.

Jesus said, "For where your treasure is, there will your heart be also" (Matthew 6:21 KJV). Through all of this, God is opening doors of opportunity to share His love. He has given the congregation a greater vision for winning souls. The people of Lakeshore Baptist Church enthusiastically pass on a message to everyone they meet: Christ is our only sure hope.

* "A Greater Vision," "Angels of Hope," and "Hidden Treasure" written with permission from Pastor Don Elbourne, Lakeshore Baptist Church, Lakeshore, Mississippi.

We Give Thee but Thine Own

We give Thee but Thine own,
Whatever the gift may be;
All that we have is Thine alone,
A trust, O Lord, from Thee.

May we Thy bounties thus
As stewards true receive,
And gladly, as Thou blessest us,
To Thee our firstfruits give. Amen.
WILLIAM WALSHAM HOW, 1823–1897

Help Me Through the Rubble

Lord, I pray for Your help in this rubble that has crashed down around me. Instead of storms of nature causing this disaster, I'm contending with a battle between good and evil. I know there are times I have brought on troubles because of my own poor choices. But this one is not of my doing.

No matter which way I turn, I see no way out. All is lost, and my hope to make things better is gone. Where is Your purpose in all this, Lord? I love You with all my heart, and I want to be used by You. But the struggles I'm going through are too great to bear.

Guide me, I pray. Help me to be in total alignment with Your will. In spite of this heartache, use me for Your glory. When the rubble in my life starts to trip me up, I pray You will lift me above the circumstances so I can be victorious for You. Help me remember how You once suffered and never became bitter. Instead, You showed compassion wherever You went.

Thank You, Lord, for helping me. When I'm bowed down with care, I praise You for Your encouragement. You are so good. You love me and never leave me alone. Thank You for providing Your angels to keep watch over me. I take comfort as You protect me from evil and harm. For You are my ever-present help—my hiding place.

Even though I'm forced to go through these things, I will not wallow in self-pity. I will not allow myself to live as though You have abandoned me. Instead, I will take the song You place on my lips and praise You with all of my heart. My hope and trust lies in You, my Savior and my God. You are my strength and portion.

Let me be a blessing to others through all this, dear Lord, so they may see Your good works through me. If one person accepts You as Savior from my reflecting You, it makes what I'm going through worthwhile. Help me hold my head up and keep a smile. For the tears I have sown, I shall reap with joy.

Why are you in despair, O my soul?
And why have you become disturbed within me?
Hope in God, for I shall yet praise Him,
The help of my countenance and my God. . . .
Be strong and let your heart take courage,
All you who hope in the LORD. . . .
And everyone who has this hope fixed on Him
    purifies himself, just as He is pure. . . .
Now may the God of hope
    fill you with all joy and peace in believing,
    so that you will abound in hope
    by the power of the Holy Spirit.

PSALM 42:11; PSALM 31:24; 1 JOHN 3:3;
        ROMANS 15:13 NASB

From Every Stormy Wind

From every stormy wind that blows,
From every swelling tide of woes,
There is a calm, a sure retreat:
'Tis found beneath the mercy seat.

There is a scene where spirits blend,
Where friend holds fellowship with friend;
Though sundered far, by faith they meet
Around one common mercy seat.

HUGH STOWELL, 1799–1865

*Hidden blessings, like gifts difficult to open,
often are of greatest value.
—It's a God-filled process!*

DIVE IN AND DRINK

The Old Home Place

Dad and I had planned the trip for several years. Since I was seven, I'd longed to see where he'd been born and raised. Instead of heroes being athletes, space commanders, or famous singers, our generation of kids admired cowboys. I always found it intriguing that my dad and his brother, Russell, were cowboys in Montana during their youth. That made them heroes in my eyes.

When I grew up, I finally had the opportunity to join Dad on a summer trip to "the old home place." The excursion took much preparation and saving of money. But the day came when we were able to strike out on our adventure. We drove to Miles City where we were joined by Russell and his wife, Dorothy. After a comfortable night's sleep in a motel, we headed forty miles out of town to a delightfully remote area called Mizpah. We were excited about what lay ahead. I was ready to dive into this adventure and drink in every memory Dad and Russell were about to share.

As we drove toward Mizpah, we exchanged busy, city traffic and smooth pavement for sporadic farms, dusty dirt roads, and slow-moving cattle that dotted the landscape. No water could be found for miles. The country in that area is cold in the winter and hot and dry during the summer.

Off to the right, we caught sight of Dad and Russell's old one-room schoolhouse. A building the size of a modest apartment had once held twelve grades of students, a coal-heated stove, and simple living quarters for their teacher. We were surprised to see the school still remained in good shape. It had been converted to a church and community building. We discovered an old pump near the school that still pulled water from a well. However, the water tasted terrible. We were glad we'd brought our own beverages.

We drove a little farther and turned east onto a long bumpy road that led to "the old home place." The log house still remained in the middle of what had once been Grandpa and Grandma's 320-acre farm. Golden hay and yellow sweet clover stretched for miles around. Blue-green sage dotted purple alfalfa fields. Shimmering cottonwood trees swayed lazily in the breeze.

We climbed from the car and walked toward the house. I took a deep breath. The air smelled clean and sweet. A cottontail rabbit darted across our path. Brown prairie dogs jumped into the hayfields and out of sight.

A startled rattlesnake chattered its warning, then retreated to the shade in the hay. The Powder River Badlands showed off their brown and gold grandeur in the far distant background.

Instead of city noise, we were able to hear the *real* world. Soft winds whispered. Crickets sang. Blackbirds, adorned with orange necks and chests, cawed enthusiastically. Soft coos came from mourning doves dressed in gray feathered attire. Delightful trills from brown and yellow meadowlarks wafted through the air and joined the feathered chorus. Somehow, I felt God had provided this display and music especially for us. More fantastic than any trips we take with our family members are the adventures awaiting us with our heavenly Father. Instead of long-planned vacations, we don't need to save money, wait for vacation time, or make reservations. Neither do we have to fly for miles. God is only a prayer away. He is ready for us to grab our Bibles and retreat with Him right now!

What wonderful blessings we experience as we read from the Bible and open our hearts to Him in prayer. How glorious it is when He anoints us with His cleansing Holy Spirit and invites us to drink from His pure, sweet living water.

Our Father guides us along our journey with Him while we remember our past. He warms our hearts as we recall the happy events. He gently helps us to release times gone by that we can no longer have and blesses us with good memories we shall always be able to cherish. When our journey of looking back brings to mind sadness, bitterness, or regret, He wraps His arms around us and gives comfort. And if we allow Him, He washes our wounds in that same living water. There, in His loving presence, He truly does restore our parched and thirsty souls.

Taste and see that the LORD is good;
blessed is the man who takes refuge in him.
PSALM 34:8 NIV

Water to Spare

Even though much of the country was dry, Dad's family was blessed with an artesian well a short walk from the house. It was a precious commodity some people didn't have. Winter or summer, the well never ran dry.

It poured into a large pond and watering trough. After sunset, wild animals used to gather around the pond to drink. We were told they still do.

During hot weather, Grandpa would open the well's pipe and flood the pond so the boys and their friends could go swimming. In the winter, he did the same. The extremely cold weather caused the pond to freeze over, and everyone went ice-skating. No matter what the season, there was always water to spare.

Dad and Russell wandered near the pond with boyish grins on their faces. They looked like they wanted to dive into the cool, clear water like days gone by. I wanted to do the same. Yet things had changed. We noticed the pipe had been shut down to a mere trickle in order to conserve water. There wasn't a big enough pond left to even consider swimming. Only enough water remained for wild animals to drink. Dad and Russell didn't think it was a good idea to shut the well down. They explained that a well is a strange thing. Unless there's a drought, the more the well is used, the more water it is capable of producing. Shutting the well down may cause it to dry up to nearly nothing.

Their family had had an open-door policy. Everyone was welcome. When neighbors needed water, Grandpa and Grandma were willing to share. Often, friends of the kids would come and stay for days or weeks at a time and help out around the place. After they finished their chores, they enjoyed jumping into the irresistible pool.

If no one was home and someone came passing through, the travelers were welcome to stop in, have a nice cool drink and a meal, always clean up their mess, and leave a little something behind for others before they moved on. Grandpa and Grandma had big hearts about helping out other people. They never knew a stranger.

Another great part of our adventure with our heavenly Father is when we're able to get away with Him and allow Him to guide our future. These breakaway times can last a few moments or several days. Somehow in our busy lives we manage to escape from outside distractions or extra sleep to a quiet spot with Him. There, again, we feed on His Word and drink from His living fountain. In doing this, He gives us the direction and certainty we so desperately need. No matter what the situation in our lives, no matter what the condition of our souls, He always welcomes us. We never come to Him as strangers. He knows us better than we know ourselves.

As we step into His presence, we soon find ourselves welcoming the peace of heart and mind our Father so freely provides. We take in a deep breath and sense His sweet, pure Spirit. In Him, we find a *real* peace and perspective for our lives. Not the peace and perspective like the world gives, but those we can obtain only through God, our Father.

Rather than our doing the talking, we learn to stop and listen. His whispers minister to our souls like the sound of the meadowlark. Certain. Clear. Irrefutable. The more we listen with our hearts, the more we hear Him assure us of His love and direction.

He really does lead us beside still waters. He really does restore our souls. He *is* the living water. Unlike the well that was shut down to almost nothing, His spiritual water flows freely to cleanse us, refill us, and give us new vitality. We aren't limited to drinking from His living water once. He welcomes us to do it again and again.

Unlike earthly waters we fear may be contaminated, the water our Father offers is pure, holy, and sweet. As He guides us, we need not fear being led in the wrong direction. We can cling to His promise that His Word (the Bible) is a lamp to our feet and a light to our path—not only leading us now, but through the rest of our lives.

Jesus answered and said to her, "Whoever drinks of this water will thirst again, but whoever drinks of the water that I shall give him will never thirst. But the water that I shall give him will become in him a fountain of water springing up into everlasting life."
JOHN 4:13–14 NKJV

Come and Drink

Are you bogged down with stress and care? Do you feel you are giving out to others spiritually more than you are taking in? Are you putting yourself last to the point where you are drained and have no more to offer? God doesn't expect us to be superheroes. In order to be spiritually healthy, we must do more than exhale. We must inhale, as well. Our strength doesn't come from within us. It comes from Christ *dwelling* within us—filling, refilling, and refueling us every day.

If we try to exist without drinking clean, fresh water, our bodies start to wither and die. In the same way, our mental and spiritual well-being doesn't do well without a fresh infilling of the Holy Spirit's life-giving water. Do more than just consider feeding on the words in the Bible and drinking of this well. Dive in! Do more than just wiggle your spiritual toes along the edges and then go your own way. Dive in and drink. Let Him fill you to the brim. When you do, He will quench your thirsty soul. He will restore your mental attitude. He will give you joy and fulfillment without limit.

Waves of Love

Here I am, Lord, at one of my favorite spots—the ocean. I am so pleased to have this breakaway. I'm grateful for my husband's best wishes and hugs when I kissed him good-bye. As You know, I've driven here to a familiar cabin so I can spend a week writing this book. A sabbatical, they call it—a special time with You.

Soon after arriving, I gravitate to the oceanfront. I look out over the endless waters. Its expanse is larger than my limited human eyesight can fathom. Neither do I comprehend its width or depth. How great You are, Lord, to create such wonder. In wisdom, You made it all.

I climb from my car, take off my shoes, and walk along the shore. One ankle has a tiny cut. No matter. When You were on this earth long ago, I imagine You removed Your sandals and waded in the shallow waters of the Sea of Galilee.

Salty ripples swirl around my feet. The soreness on my ankle surprisingly disappears. The salt water feels soothing and cleansing. I want to pause and lie down along the water's edge and bask in the sun. Still, I'm keenly aware of the elements of danger. If I mindlessly neglect Your rules of nature, the same water could crash in around me with waves of deadly force as solid and high as a brick wall.

When I ignore the instructions You give for my life, different kinds of storms catch me unaware. It is then You remind me that You are more powerful than any tempest I'm facing and that I need not fear. For You have charge over the uncertain seas of my life. Amazingly, You set my feet on firm ground and help right my paths.

When I ponder the depths of this vast ocean, You help me recall how You listen to my repentant prayers and bury my sins in the deepest part of the sea. Amazingly, You remove my transgressions from me and cast them out, as far as the east is from the west. Thank You for the waves of Your merciful love.

Thank You for Your glorious creation, Lord. I breathe deeply and feel the salty air clearing my sinuses. Thank You for how this much-needed salt water doesn't evaporate as quickly as regular water. The salt makes the waves move as though they have a life of their own. How amazing is this ocean that helps regulate our weather system—the moon and tides synchronize in perfect harmony.

I walk a little farther and gingerly step around ugly, brown scum floating in with the tide. I'm told this is algae. Thank You for it, too. Its nutrients feed tiny critters like the sea shrimp, clams, and sand dollars.

There's a sand dollar, Lord, hiding in a shallow pool. The legend about it causes me to meditate on Your holy Trinity—God, the Father; God, the Son; and God, the Holy Spirit. Your sovereignty is indescribable. This fantastic creation can't begin to compare to You.

Thank You for the families running and playing games together. Colorful kites dance in the wind. How graceful are the seagulls as they soar and dive, gliding on the air currents. I watch an older couple don their coats and hats, then walk hand in hand along the beach. These are their sunset years. These are the years they are still blessed with life, Your love, and each other.

It's getting late, Lord. Hunger gnaws at my stomach. Still, I'm not ready to leave. I want to remain a little longer and watch the sun set. I want to enjoy more time in this special place to commune with You.

Hundreds of petite gray-and-white-spotted sandpipers feed on the bugs, then ribbon their way through the air in perfect order. The sun slowly sinks toward the western horizon. The water shimmers from the reflection of its rays. Kites are reeled in. Families leave to settle in for the evening. The elderly couple is silhouetted by the sun. Their shadows lengthen on the glistening sand. They stroll back to their car and drive away. The beach is almost empty. Even the seagulls are becoming quiet. Everything takes on a different feeling. It's one of tranquillity—a preparation for nightfall and rest.

I turn and walk back toward my car and watch the sea caps and horizon turn silver. I glance to the east and marvel at the vivid turquoise sky. A full moon steadily rises and bids the sun adieu. When I reach my car and climb in, I notice a new group of people quietly parking their cars along the beach. They have lined up, facing the water, as though they are ready to watch an outdoor movie. This sunset, however, is real, and is giving the grandest and most stunning performance of all.

I sit and watch, quietly singing praises to You of Your mighty love. I come to You, unafraid, as Your sweet Spirit surrounds me and fills my soul. Greater than the abundance of this ocean stretching from north to south, Your stream of living water fills me to the brim. It soothes my heart and heals my hurts. It washes over and cleanses me.

The sun sinks low enough to nearly blind my view. The sky changes from silver to soft amber to bright yellow. Soon after, the entire horizon turns a brilliant mixture of blues and various shades of orange. A big, red ball puts on its final flamboyant performance, then stealthily disappears behind the ocean waves.

Thank You for giving me peace of heart, for calming my emotions, for taking my concerns on Your shoulders. As I bring the needs of my loved ones and friends to You, I praise You for being with them. Thank You for giving me strength for this day and hope for tomorrow. Thank You, Lord, for washing me with Your waves of love. Remain with me, I pray, as I return to my cabin and rest in You.

"The LORD will continually guide you,
And satisfy your desire in scorched places,
And give strength to your bones;
And you will be like a watered garden,
And like a spring of water whose waters do not
    fail." . . .
[Your children will] drink their fill of the abun-
    dance of Your house. . . .
You give them to drink of the river of Your
    delights.
For with You is the fountain of life. . . .
For thus says the LORD, "Behold, I extend
    peace. . .like a river. . .like an overflowing
    stream." . . .
Now on the last day, the great day of the feast,
Jesus stood and cried out, saying,
"If anyone is thirsty, let him come to Me and
    drink.
"He who believes in Me, as the Scripture said,
'From his innermost being will flow rivers of
    living water.'"

ISAIAH 58:11; PSALM 36:8–9;
ISAIAH 66:12; JOHN 7:37–38 NASB

Waves of Devotion

A glorious blessing bestowed upon me
Salvation the joy of my heart!
The theme of my song and forever shall be,
To me Thy rich graces impart.

My pathway is bright as the cloudless noonday,
My peace like a river that flows;
Upon me such blessings are showered always,
Which grace in profusion bestows.

The waves of devotion are flooding my soul,
And sparkle so bright in the sun;
I drink of that fountain, O glory, I'm whole!
My Eden on earth has begun.

BARNEY ELLIOTT WARREN, 1867–1951

The purest drink comes not from filtered
water or a clear, rippling stream.
The purest drink comes from God's well
of living water that shall never run dry.
—It's a God-filled process!

Mary and Martha

A Better Way

The Bible tells about two close friends of Jesus—Mary and Martha. They were sisters. Their personalities were as different as night and day. However, they both loved the Lord with all their hearts.

The sisters were most likely very excited about Jesus coming to visit them. Each did all she could to make Him feel welcome. They wanted to take advantage of the time they would have together.

Martha probably made sure every nook and cranny was spotless. She bustled around, preparing a meal for her Savior that was fit for a king. She may have spent several days getting ready for Jesus' visit. Perhaps she grew tired and somewhat irritable. (Do we ever get that way?)

After Jesus arrived, Martha kept scurrying about, worrying over the little things. Mary, on the other hand, simply sat quietly at her Savior's feet and listened intently to everything He said. Martha probably wanted to join in on their visit. But her preparation of the meal was already well into full swing.

She may have felt overworked and left out. She bristled at the thought of Mary leaving her with all that needed to be done.

Finally, Martha interrupted Jesus and Mary's conversation: "She came to him and asked, 'Lord, don't you care that my sister has left me to do the work by myself? Tell her to help me!'" (Luke 10:40 NIV). Jesus may have looked at her and sighed. " 'Martha, Martha,' the Lord answered, 'you are worried and upset about many things, but only one thing is needed. Mary has chosen what is better, and it will not be taken away from her'" (Luke 10:41–42 NIV).

Jesus wanted Martha's love and attention more than anything. Do you wonder if she ever learned a better way?

Opposites for God

Another Martha* and her husband, Tim, wholeheartedly served in the ministry of their church. They, too, were as different as night and day. Martha was filled with an abundance of energy and enthusiasm. Whenever there was a need, she jumped in with both feet. She organized potlucks; planned retreats; took time cleaning the church sanctuary, the kitchen, and even the bathrooms. Most of all, she enjoyed sending cards of encouragement to those who needed them and taking flowers or a hot dish to shut-ins.

However, Martha wasn't like her namesake in the Bible. She looked forward to awakening early in the morning so she could enjoy a quiet time with her Lord. She carefully scheduled her day to accomplish what she felt God was leading her to do. After much trial and error, she learned to remain aware of when the Lord was telling her to slow down.

Unlike Martha, Tim was quiet and laid-back. He loved to dream and ponder. Sermons, Bible study ideas, and songs he loved to write constantly whirred in his mind. He never seemed in a hurry when someone wanted to share their concerns and needs with him. No matter what the situation, he would say, "Let's stop and pray about this."

Sometimes Martha became frustrated with her husband. She wished he would help her more with the church projects. Tim would look at her hustling around and simply state, "Honey, why don't you just sit down for a while?"

One day a man they knew became seriously ill. Tim and Martha hurried to the hospital to be with him and his family. Tim sat by the man's bedside and quietly prayed. Martha comforted the family in the waiting room and prayed with them. She brought the anxious family members tea from the cafeteria and kept them company so they wouldn't feel so alone.

It was during this time that Tim and Martha realized that although they were opposites in personality, they really did complement each other. God had given them each an important gift to use in serving Him. Martha appreciated Tim's calm, empathetic spirit. She wondered what life would be like without wonderful people like him. Tim breathed a sigh of relief, knowing Martha was handling the little things that needed to be done while he remained by his friend's bedside. He wondered what life would be like without wonderful people like her.

Rather than trying to change each other, the couple grew to be more accepting of their individual personalities and God-given gifts. With God as their central focus, they had genuinely become a team in service for Him.

*Names changed.

Patience in Retreat

Patience is hard, sometimes. Whilst I am climbing the mountains, passing through the wilderness, daring dangers, I feel comparatively quiet, or even glad. But to sit down when the angel tells me to sit, and not to stir till He comes back again—who can do it?

Make the best of your leisure. It is for a wise purpose. Gather strength, let the brain sleep, yield yourself to the spirit of the quietness of God, and after what appears to be wasted time or unprofitable waiting, there shall come an inspiration into the soul that shall make thee strong and fearless.

JOSEPH PARKER, 1830–1902

I Want to Be Like You

There are so many different personalities in Your family, Lord. Some, I really enjoy. Others, however, rub against my grain and cause me to grind my teeth. I know this isn't the way You want me to be. Please help me to change my attitude, Lord. Help me to recognize the love You have for each of us.

Thank You for making us different and giving us spiritual gifts and talents in accordance with Your will. Show me how we can help and appreciate each other more in being part of Your family. How boring it would be if everyone were just like me.

I want to be like You, Lord. Lead me in the way You choose for me to go. Guide me with Your counsel. Let me hide Your Word in my heart so I don't become critical and sin against You.

I love You, Lord, with all my heart, my soul, and my mind. Help me to be a member of Your family, who lives wholeheartedly in accordance with Your will. Instead of wanting things my way, I ask You to help me love and care for others as You love and care for me.

None of Self and All of Thee

O the bitter shame and sorrow,
That a time could ever be,
When I let the Savior's pity
Plead in vain, and proudly answered,
"All of self, and none of Thee!"

Yet He found me; I beheld Him
Bleeding on th'accursèd tree,
Heard Him pray, "Forgive them, Father!"
And my wistful heart said faintly,
"Some of self, and some of Thee!"

Day by day His tender mercy,
Healing, helping, full and free,
Sweet and strong, and ah! so patient,
Brought me lower, while I whispered,
"Less of self, and more of Thee!"

Higher than the highest heaven,
Deeper than the deepest sea,
Lord, Thy love at last has conquered,
None of self, and all of Thee.
THEODORE MONAD, 1836–1921

We have different gifts, according to the grace given us. If a man's gift is prophesying, let him use it in proportion to his faith. If it is serving, let him serve; if it is teaching, let him teach; if it is encouraging, let him encourage; if it is contributing to the needs of others, let him give generously; if it is leadership, let him govern diligently; if it is showing mercy, let him do it cheerfully.

Love must be sincere. Hate what is evil; cling to what is good. Be devoted to one another in brotherly love. Honor one another above yourselves. Never be lacking in zeal, but keep your spiritual fervor, serving the Lord.

ROMANS 12:6–11 NIV

The Model Church

Well, wife, I've found the model church,
    and worshipped there today.
It made me think of good old times,
    before my hair was gray.
The meeting house was finer built
    than they were years ago;
But then I found when I went in,
    it was not built for show.

The sexton did not set me down
    away back by the door.
He knew that I was old and deaf
    and saw that I was poor.
He must have been a Christian man.
    He led me boldly through
The crowded aisle of that grand church
    to find a pleasant pew.

I wish you'd heard the singing, wife.
    It had the old-time ring.
The preacher said with trumpet voice,
    "Let all the people sing!"
"All Hail the Power!" was the hymn.
    The music upward rolled,
Until I thought the angel choir struck
    all their harps of gold.

My deafness seemed to melt away,
    my spirit caught the fire.
I joined my feeble, trembling voice,
    with that melodious choir.
And sang, as in my youthful days,
    "Let angels prostrate fall!
"Bring forth the royal diadem,
    and crown Him Lord of all!"

'Twas not a flowery sermon, wife,
    but simple gospel truth.
It fitted humble men like me.
    It suited hopeful youth.
To win immortal souls to Christ,
    the earnest preacher tried.
He talked not of himself, or creed,
    but Jesus crucified!

JOHN H. YATES, 1837–1900

Do all the good you can,
By all the means you can,
In all the ways you can,
In all the places you can,
At all the times you can,
To all the people you can,
As long as ever you can.
JOHN WESLEY, 1703–1791

—It's a God-filled process!

CHURCH CPR

Where Are the Answered Prayers?

A handful of five or six people stood in front of the small church building. These people felt God was leading them to start a new congregation in this very place. But they wondered how the Lord would make it possible. The building was filled with junk and rotten garbage. In some places, the trash almost reached the ceiling. More rubbish spilled out into the parking lot and under the front steps. How sad it was to see a house of God being treated this way.

The people didn't know where the money would come from to rent the building. They trusted the Lord for that. God had led them there, and He would make a way. Amazingly, enough tithes and offerings came in each month to supply their need. They visualized their new congregation reaching families in the neighborhood. Each week they met in the only clean area of the church—the sanctuary. Each week they cleaned and prayed that God would answer their prayers.

Everyone rolled up his and her sleeves and continued cleaning more vigorously than ever. The workers took load after load of trash to the local dump. When they finally finished hauling the garbage away, they estimated the total exceeded over three tons. Sadly, they learned the building had been used previously in sinful activities. Whenever anyone walked in the church doors, a strange sense of sadness was felt. The reputation of the church had to be restored. The small group of people continued to clean, scrub, and pray.

Soon, local businessmen and women and residents living near the church noticed the improvements. One by one, they dropped by and offered their encouragement. Whenever the congregation needed something for its church, it was provided. God was already answering the people's prayers.

One morning after the worship service, the group decided to dedicate the building to the Lord. The pastor took his small bottle of olive oil as the congregation prepared to pray more fervently than ever. They went from room to room, anointing the doors with oil and asking God to fill each room with His cleansing Holy Spirit. There wasn't any great emotion or a mighty rushing wind. The people simply trusted God to accept their dedication.

One week passed. Two weeks. At the end of the second week, a feeling of pure joy and freedom filled the place. Unmistakably, it was the holy presence of the Lord. The promise from God in Haggai 2:19, "From this day I will bless you" (NKJV), was ringing true.

Shortly after, a lady came to worship who had visited the church years before. The first thing she mentioned was how she sensed a different feeling when she walked through the door. She, too, felt the Holy Spirit's glorious presence.

To the surprise of the group, the church building became available for purchase. How would this be possible? The members of the group wouldn't question. God had led them there, and He would make a way. And He did. From the beginning, they were able to make their payments and to get them in on time.

The congregation continued to pray for God to reach the community. Everyone visualized a nice little family church. But God had more than that planned. Along with reaching families in the neighborhood, He brought in the injured and disabled; those who had been and were being abused; those recovering from alcohol and drugs.

This time, the people prayed for help and for lives to be encouraged and changed. They started some exciting Sunday school classes for children and youth. Those who suffered mercilessly turned their lives over to God and were healed. Many saw hope for their future. Adults found jobs. Families grew closer. Youngsters learned how to cope with and be victorious over the difficult circumstances they were forced to deal with.

After services, clusters of people remained. They visited in the sanctuary and dining room—listening, caring, and praying for one another's needs. Genuine care and love were filling the place! God was performing a holy CPR on His people. The congregation had become a spiritual hospital. It didn't matter whether they were rich or poor, disabled or injured. No one looked down their noses or sized people up. Everyone was welcome.

The church vibrated with activity. In addition to its own congregation worshipping there, other groups used the building. A Spanish-speaking congregation came in. A motorcycle ministry met on Sunday nights. One evening a week, another group came that helped people get off drugs and alcohol.

Where were the answers to the little group's prayers to have a church for the community? They were being answered. God sent hurting people from not only the neighborhood, but also from miles away. Each grew to love and help the other. They *became* the church—the family of God.

[Jesus said,] "Inasmuch as you did it to one of the least of these My brethren, you did it to Me."
MATTHEW 25:40 NKJV

Birds in the Attic

The congregation didn't stop there. There were fist-sized holes in the roof. Again, God supplied the church's need. Money came in to put a new roof on the building and make some major repairs. Young and old pitched in and landscaped. They painted the outside of the church building white with gray trim. It was beginning to stand out in the community as a sparkling landmark.

One of their more challenging projects involved climbing into the attic to clean out the birds' nests. Although everyone loved the birds, the job had to be done. What a smelly job it was! Bag after bag of old nests was passed down the ladder and taken to the garbage can. Fortunately, they cleaned house before the spring eggs were laid. New screens were put in. The birds had to find homes elsewhere.

With God's help, the congregation cleansed and rebuilt His temple—His dwelling place.

In the same way that God urged this little group to clean and restore the church building, He encourages us to do so with our minds, bodies, and souls. When we're willing to yield to Him, God restores us and guides us in the right way. He gives us strength to get rid of the garbage and debris from the birds' nests we have allowed to clog our lives. The Bible says we are meant to be His temple.

It takes a lot of work to do serious personal house-cleaning. We must invite Jesus in and allow Him to fill every room. When we do, amazing changes take place. Our shame and discouragement are replaced with forgiveness and hope that comes only from the Savior. Instead of being lost and confused, we begin to experience His infinite love and direction. It is then that we can buckle our spiritual seat belts and hang on for a ride with Him, filled with marvelous life-changing experiences and blessings.

Do you not know that you are the temple of God and that the Spirit of God dwells in you?
1 CORINTHIANS 3:16 NKJV

Your Everlasting Church

I come to You, Lord, here in a little ocean-side town—Copalis, Washington. I'm meeting in a community church with a group of ladies I've just met. Even though I'm a stranger, these women welcome me into their fellowship. As we study Your Word and pray for one another and our families, I feel a part of them. For we are all one family—Your family, Lord.

Thank You for Your church. Whether there are two or eight in a Bible study group or a huge congregation meeting in a sanctuary, You are in the midst. I read in Ephesians that we are no longer strangers or foreigners. We are members of God's very own family.

Thank You for being the head of the church. Thank You for making all who believe members of Your church, the body of Christ. In gratefulness and humility, we become this marvelous church's hands and feet. Let everything we say and do stir up love and kindness. May we always uplift and encourage one another.

Praise You, dear Lord, for Your everlasting church. No matter what it has gone through in the past, no matter what it may face in the future, Your church is triumphant. It remains true and strong here on earth and shall continue to live triumphantly in heaven. Praise You, O Lord! Praise You for Your holy church now and through eternity. Amen and amen!

[Jesus said,] "For where two or three are gathered together in my name, there am I in the midst of them." . . .

[Jesus said,] "Upon this rock I will build my church; and the gates of hell shall not prevail against it." . . .

"For you are a holy people to the LORD your God, and the LORD has chosen you to be a people for Himself, a special treasure above all the peoples who are on the face of the earth." . . .

For we are members of His body, of His flesh and of His bones.

MATTHEW 18:20; 16:18 KJV; DEUTERONOMY 14:2; EPHESIANS 5:30 NKJV

Once Again We Come

Once again we come to the house of God,
To unite in songs of praise;
To extol with joy our Redeemer's name,
And to tell His works and ways.

In our days gone by, Thou hast been our stay,
Thou hast led us safely on
To the blessed light of the present day,
Where the darkness now is gone.

May our hearts, O Lord, e'er united be
In true fellowship and love;
May Thy will be done by us here on earth,
As by angel hosts above.

CHARLES W. NAYLOR, 1874–1950

Every Task However Simple

Every task, however simple,
sets the soul that does it free;
Every deed of love and kindness,
done to man is done to Thee.
HENRY VAN DYKE, 1852–1933

—It's a God-filled process!

LIFE AFTER LIFE

What Will Heaven Be Like?

Do you ever wonder what heaven will be like? Do you long for relief from the discord and heartache, the stress and uncertainty that propels your life into uncontrollable turmoil? Does your fast-paced world ever shift into overdrive to the point where you wish you could press the STOP button—or at least put it on PAUSE? When struck with pain and suffering, do you long for more than temporary relief? Although we have a built-in passion to love this earthly life, many of us who know Jesus as our Savior look forward to the day we will be with Him in heaven.

Do you feel you're being left behind when a loved one goes on to that glorious place before you? In heaven, there will no tears. No sickness or grief. No separation from the ones we here on earth now miss.

Heaven will be better than an old-fashioned camp meeting. It will be better than a two- or three-day retreat. It will even be better than those precious, intimate times when the air is so thick with His presence that we feel we can almost touch Him. In heaven, we *will* be able to touch Him! There will be a never-ending, holy camp meeting. We will always enjoy His glorious presence. There will be no late or early hours—no time limits.

In the same way Paul was delivered from shackles, the strife we are forced to contend with here shall be no more. Long- and short-term illnesses and pain will be replaced with immortality and eternal health. Instead of praying for Jesus to still the turmoil in our lives, those storms will be gone in the twinkling of an eye. There will be no sin—just perfect love. All the stress, all the anxiety, all the fear of being hurt or deceived will vanish. We shall find in their place wonderful, perfect peace.

I imagine when we get to heaven, we will hear the glorious music of angels and saints praising God. One by one, we will be reunited with the loved ones who are waiting for us.

And our unanswered questions? I don't believe we'll even have to ask them. The dim vision we now have to contend with on earth will become clear. In heaven, there will be comfort, certainty, and all the answers we need.

How incredible it will be to enter the presence of our heavenly Father, His Son, and the Holy Spirit. We shall finally meet the Savior face-to-face. What a beautiful face we'll behold! Will we feel worthy enough to stand in His presence? Or will we be so overwhelmed that we fall prostrate before Him, barely able to lift our heads?

Either way, I can visualize Him taking our hands, looking into our eyes, and saying, "Your sins have been forgiven, My children. Welcome home."

And in the end, it's not the years in your life that count.
It's the life in your years.
ABRAHAM LINCOLN, 1809–1865

The sweetest music is not the peal of marriage bells, nor tender descants in moonlight wood, nor trumpet notes of victory—it is the soul's welcome to heaven. God grant that when we die there may not come booming to our ear the dreadful sound, "Depart!" But may we hear stealing upon the air the mellow chime of all the celestial bells saying, "Come, come, come, ye blessed, enter ye into the joy of the Lord!"

Henry Ward Beecher, 1813–1887

A Homesick Feeling

Father, when I think of heaven, I get a homesick feeling. I love my life here on earth with my husband, family, and friends. But there's a side of me that longs to be with You in that glorious place. There's a familiar feeling about it, as though I'll someday be coming home.

I dream of meeting You face-to-face, my glorious Savior. I look forward to being reunited with my loved ones. Yet I'm grateful that You ease my yearning to be with You there, and fill me with Your comforting presence. For You *are* with me all the time, every day. You, Lord, are in charge of the big picture and know how long You want me to live on this earth. Thank You for the perfect plans You have for my life.

When You're ready to take me home, I'll be anxiously waiting for You. In the meantime, let me be a blessing in every way I can. Grant me patience through good and bad experiences. Keep within my heart a deep-down joy and peace that can only come from You.

I [John] heard a loud voice from heaven saying, "Behold. . . God will wipe away every tear from their eyes; there shall be no more death, nor sorrow, nor crying. There shall be no more pain, for the former things have passed away." . . .

Then I looked, and I heard the voice of many angels around the throne, the living creatures, and the elders; and the number of them was ten thousand times ten thousand, and thousands of thousands, saying with a loud voice:

"Worthy is the Lamb who was slain
To receive power and riches and wisdom,
And strength and honor and glory and blessing!"

And every creature which is in heaven and on the earth and under the earth and such as are in the sea, and all that are in them, I heard saying:

"Blessing and honor and glory and power
Be to Him who sits on the throne,
And to the Lamb, forever and ever!"

REVELATION 21:3–4; 5:11–13 NKJV

Ten Thousand Times Ten Thousand

Ten thousand times ten thousand,
In sparkling raiment bright,
The armies of the ransomed saints
Throng up the steeps of light;
'Tis finished—all is finished,
Their fight with death and sin!
Fling open wide the golden gates,
And let the victors in!

What rush of "Hallelujahs"
Fills all the earth and sky!
What ringing of a thousand harps
Bespeaks the triumph nigh!
O day, for which creation
And all its tribes were made!
Oh, joy! For all its former woes
A thousandfold repaid!

Oh, then what raptured greetings
On Canaan's happy shore!
What knitting severed friendships up,
Where partings are no more!
Then eyes of joy shall sparkle,
That brimmed with tears of late;
No longer, orphans, fatherless,
Nor widows desolate.

Hallelujah! Hallelujah
To the Lamb who was slain!
Hallelujah! Hallelujah
To Him who lives again!

HENRY ALFORD, 1810–1871

I paid the price and set you free,
So you may someday live with Me.
—It truly is a God-filled process!

HARMONY WITH GOD

How Shall I Be Remembered?

When my years are spent and I leave this earthly body to meet You in heaven, how shall I be remembered, Lord? Will those who have known me think of me as being gracious and caring? Will they remember my successes and failures? My good looks? (I don't think so.) Will they gather in anticipation of the huge fortune I might leave behind? (If so, they may be sorely disappointed!)

It doesn't matter, Lord, if I am rich or famous during my life. These things are only temporary. However, it *does* matter to me how people will recall my attitudes. More important is what kind of life I have exhibited to others.

Help me live in harmony with Your desires and plans for me. Show me the way to be a good example for those who follow in my path. When I fall short, I ask for Your forgiveness. Help me to right my wrongs. Guide me in the ways You want me to go.

I want to leave a legacy of faithfulness to You for those I love and brush shoulders with each day. Bless me with the ability to reflect You in my attitude, especially when things aren't going my way. I want to be thought of as one who views the cup half full, rather than half empty. I want those who know me to recall Your unselfishness and holiness that I seek and long to dwell within me.

I feel unworthy of being Your servant, Lord. There is no way I can reflect this holy life without Your cleansing Spirit. Mold me, I pray. Refine all my ways so they become pleasing to You.

Orchestrate my life to be in complete harmony with Your will, dear Lord. Make me an example for my family and friends, so they will receive strength and inspiration to carry them through their future years.

How shall I be remembered? Rather than their thinking of me, let them keep in mind You who paid the price for each one of us. From You, Lord, came all!

Blessed is every one who fears the LORD,
Who walks in His ways.
When you eat the labor of your hands,
You shall be happy, and it shall be well with you. . . .
In the very heart of your house,
Your children [shall be] like olive plants
All around your table.
Behold, thus shall the man [or woman] be blessed
Who fears the LORD.
PSALM 128:1–4 NKJV

Light tomorrow with today.
ELIZABETH BARRETT BROWNING, 1806–1861

God-Appointed Phone Call

Rob sat in the morning church service where he came to worship almost every Sunday. On that particular morning, his pastor began preaching a memorable message called "Catching a Dream"—a message Rob will most likely never forget. He was waiting for a phone call involving a dream of his own.

Normally, Rob would have turned his cell phone off during the service. But this one was important. And he didn't want to miss church. Besides, everyone in the congregation had been keeping him in prayer.

The phone rang. The service stopped. Rob answered. It was Mike Holmgren, the Seattle Seahawks coach.

"Turn up the volume on your television, Rob."

"Um, I can't. I'm in church."

There, among his church family, he found out he was chosen to play for the Seahawks. He had been praying he would get picked. Now God was blessing him.

There was something even better than Rob's answered prayer. Through the phone call, he unknowingly showed football fans everywhere how he keeps his life in harmony with God. Although football is one of the most important things to him, God comes first.

God bless you, Rob! Keep playing for the Lord.

The Redwood Cathedral

It was an unusually warm November in northern California. Bob and I were on our way home from a great Thanksgiving visit with our son and daughter-in-law, Jonathan and Cynthia. The inviting sunshine enticed us to take a detour and drive along the Pacific Coast. One of our priorities was to travel through the redwood forest.

We spotted the signs directing us to Humboldt Redwoods State Park and turned onto a lesser-traveled road. Trees larger than any we had ever seen lined our route. Branches draped a thick canopy over us. Even though it was day, they darkened the way so much that we had to turn on our car lights. We felt as though we had entered a redwood cathedral.

Great is the LORD, and greatly to be praised; and his greatness is unsearchable.

PSALM 145:3 KJV

We pulled up to the Redwood Forest Information Center and found someone who happily took us on a tour. Our guide wasted no time telling the secrets of the redwoods. As we walked through the huge forest, we felt awestruck. A thick layer of giant sequoia needles covered the ground and made it softer to walk on than our living room carpet. The guide pointed out that the giant sequoia—or "Big Tree"—ranks as one of the world's oldest tree types. Some redwoods are estimated to be as much as 2,500 years old and surpass 350 feet in height. That's equivalent to a thirty-five-story building. They are estimated to weigh about 1,800 tons per acre! The oldest known sequoia redwood has fallen now with about 3,300 annual growth rings.

O give thanks to. . .him who alone doeth great wonders: for his mercy endureth for ever.

PSALM 136:3–4 KJV

When the guide explained how important the sequoias are to our environment, it left an impact on me. The Pacific Coast gives off a fog that helps protect the trees from cold and heat. In turn, the redwoods generate some of their own fog that condenses at night above the treetops and makes a form of rain. A large redwood can release as much as 500 gallons of water into the air each day.

Bless the LORD, O my soul. . . . Who layeth the beams of his chambers in the waters: who maketh the clouds his chariot: who walketh upon the wings of the wind.

PSALM 104:1, 3 KJV

We asked the guide to take our picture in front of a redwood tree. He directed us to one over 2,000 years old. It was approximately 270 feet tall and 30 feet thick at the trunk's base. Its weight is estimated at over a million pounds. When he showed us the other side of the tree, we gasped. A forest fire had left huge black marks on its bark and a six-foot hollow in its trunk. Since the redwood bark is very hard and contains no pitch, the trees often fend off fires, as this one did. There, we had our picture taken. We must have looked like two tiny straight pins next to something so gigantic.

Great is our Lord, and of great power: his understanding is infinite.

PSALM 147:5 KJV

The most amazing thing we learned about redwoods is how they depend upon each other. They have shallow root systems that extend only three to six feet beneath the ground. Roots from surrounding trees connect with each other and form a type of trampoline. This helps stabilize the trees from wind and flood, and balances their weight so they remain upright. The top branches of the redwoods lace the trees together like clasped hands. They form a canopy, protecting the trees and wildlife from harsh winters and summers.

Who hath measured the waters in the hollow of his hand, and meted out heaven with the span, and comprehended the dust of the earth in a measure, and weighed the mountains in scales, and the hills in a balance?

ISAIAH 40:12 KJV

Bob and I thanked our guide for his wealth of information. We drove away feeling grateful for how God blesses by putting together this enormous miracle of nature.

For ye shall go out with joy, and be led forth with peace: the mountains and the hills shall break forth before you into singing, and all the trees of the field shall clap their hands.

ISAIAH 55:12 KJV

Imagine how much more God wants to work His intricate plans of harmony through us. He provides us with a gift far more valuable than this tangible creation here on earth. His gift is our remarkable Christian family. It has no limit in numbers or geographical boundaries.

Unlike the redwoods' shallow roots, God encourages us to sink our roots deeply into Him. He is the foundation of our spiritual existence. As He feeds and waters our souls, He wants us to stretch our roots and branches out and help hold one another up through love, deed, and prayer.

We are the church—brothers and sisters in the Lord. Those we share a common bond of God's love with may be by our side or on the other side of the world. We rejoice with those who rejoice. We weep with those who hurt. When we face the fiery trials of persecution, temptation, vigorous spiritual battles, discouragement, and sometimes mourning, we pull together and strengthen each other in the name of Jesus Christ.

There's power in God's church. No matter what the circumstances, this blessed family of God triumphs now, and shall be victorious forever.

Now here is what I am trying to say: All of you together are the one body of Christ and each one of you is a separate and necessary part of it....

All of you, live in harmony with one another; be sympathetic, love as brothers, be compassionate and humble....

Be joyful in hope, patient in affliction, faithful in prayer....

Rejoice with those who rejoice; mourn with those who mourn....

1 CORINTHIANS 12:27 TLB; 1 PETER 3:8;
ROMANS 12:12, 15 NIV

Messenger of Hope

He lived in his quiet, beloved home in Africa and wanted to stay there for the rest of his life. Money was hard to come by during this time. In order to survive, he found it necessary to leave Africa and play the organ at Westminster Abbey. Crowds gathered from miles around to listen to his glorious music. Before long, he gained fame as the greatest organist in Europe. Along with his own musical accomplishments, he grew to be an authority on the life and work of composer Johann Sebastian Bach. But he didn't stop there. In addition to being a famous musician, he turned out to be a renowned theologian. He produced several volumes on religious subjects. He could have remained in Europe and enjoyed his fame as a musician and theologian, but God had other plans for him.

As a boy, he loved to hear missionary stories. As an adult, he felt haunted by the afflictions natives in Africa had to endure. What they were going through tore at his heart. How could he make a difference? He knew God was calling him to return to Africa and help them. Fame, money, and personal comforts paled in comparison with what he knew God wanted him to do. No matter how high the cost, he gave his all to God and His will. In order to be as much help to the African people as possible, he decided to study medicine and become a physician and surgeon.

Universities and cities in Europe gave him numerous honors for his accomplishments. Still, he never lost sight of his call to serve in Africa.

In 1913 he was finally able to return to his beloved Africa as a physician. His wife, who was a nurse, went with him. A hospital was built. People were helped physically and spiritually by the couple's faithful work. At times he had to stand against the world in order to accomplish what God had led him to do. This caused a great deal of turmoil. Even his friends were appalled at his position. Still, nothing deterred his commitment to God's call.

In 1931, he took a "vacation" in Europe, wrote another book, performed concerts, and raised money for the hospital in Africa. Just before Christmas, he returned to Africa and continued his work in the hospital and helping people.

Those he served developed a sincere love for him. The African people affectionately called him Ogangua of the Forest.

The sincere and unswerving confession of Albert Schweitzer's faith was that he faithfully shared his love for God and Christianity through all his years, even though he longed to "practice Christianity silently."

What a wonderful example he was of being in harmony with God and His will!

If Thou but Suffer God to Guide Thee

If thou but suffer God to guide thee,
And hope in Him through all thy ways,
He'll give thee strength, whate'er betide thee,
And bear thee through the evil days.
Who trusts in God's unchanging love
Builds on the rock that naught can move.

Only be still and wait His leisure
In cheerful hope, with heart content
To take whate'er thy Father's pleasure
And all-deserving love hath sent,
Nor doubt our inmost wants are known
To Him who chose us for His own.

Sing, pray, and keep His ways unswerving,
So do thine own part faithfully,
And trust His Word, though undeserving;
Thou yet shall find it true for thee;
God never yet forsook at need
The soul that trusted Him indeed. Amen.

GEORG NEUMARK, 1621–1681
TRANSLATED BY CATHERINE WINKWORTH,
1827–1878

Harmony with You

How wonderful You are, O Lord. Your majesty surpasses all else. Thank You for being my Counselor and Comforter, my mighty God. What assurance I have in Your love, because You are my Father—my Abba Father. My heavenly Daddy. My Papa. You are King of Kings and Lord of Lords! How blessed I am for Your being my Savior and setting me free from sin. I simply can't understand why You saw fit to bless me with Your faithful, everlasting love. Without You, dreams and efforts are of no value.

Take this life of mine. Touch me. Fill me with Your holy presence. Use me. Let me be in harmony with You in all my ways. With my mouth I offer acclamation to You, dear Lord. My songs exalt You. I lift my hands and give You glory and honor. Let all that is within me bless Your holy name.

To You be all glory and power forever and ever! Amen.

The LORD is my strength and my shield;
my heart trusts in him, and I am helped.
My heart leaps for joy
and I will give thanks to him in song.
PSALM 28:7 NIV

Obedience

I said, "Let me walk in the field."
He said, "No, walk in the town."
I said, "There are no flowers there."
He said, "No flowers, but a crown."

I said, "But the sky is black; there is
nothing but noise and din."
And He wept as He sent me back,
"There is more," He said. "There is sin."

I said, "But the air is thick, and fogs are
veiling the sun."
He answered, "Yet souls are sick and
souls in the dark undone."

I said, "I shall miss the light, and friends
will miss me, they say."
He answered me, "Choose tonight, if I
am to miss you, or they."

I pleaded for time to be given;
He said, "Is it hard to decide?
It will not seem hard in Heaven to have
followed the steps of your Guide."

I cast one look at the fields,
Then set my face to the town;
He said, "My child, do you yield? Will
you leave the flowers for the crown?"

Then into His hand went mine,
And into my heart came He;
And I walk in a light Divine,
The path I had feared to see.
   GEORGE MACDONALD, 1824–1905

Bless the LORD, O my soul:
and all that is within me,
bless his holy name.
Bless the LORD, O my soul,
and forget not all his benefits:
Who forgiveth all thine iniquities;
who healeth all thy diseases;
Who redeemeth thy life from destruction;
who crowneth thee with lovingkindness
and tender mercies;
Who satisfieth thy mouth with good things;
so that thy youth is renewed like the eagle's.
PSALM 103:1–5 KJV

Heartsong

I want to write a song for you
And offer You my praise.
I want to sing it pure and clear,
My thankfulness to raise.

I want to wrap it up in love
And fling it to the sky,
Where you can catch my offering
When it goes floating by.

My all, my life, my will to You
I gratefully impart;
Yet more than any offering
I give to You my heart.

No other song is lovelier than the
one God pens upon the heart.
—It's a God-filled process.

May God's favor shine upon you as you go about your day.
May your thoughts be bright, your feet be sure.
May you be mindful of His promise:

"From this day, I will bless you" (Haggai 2:19 NKJV).